READY**SET**
KNIT

LEARN TO KNIT WITH **20** HOT PROJECTS

SASHA KAGAN

Creative Publishing
international

First published in 2004 in the USA and Canada by Creative Publishing international, Inc.

Creative Publishing
international

18705 Lake Drive East
Chanhassen Minnesota 55317
1-800-328-3895
www.creativepub.com

First published in UK in 2004 by
Carroll & Brown Publishers
20 Lonsdale Road
Queens Park
London NW6 6RD

Project Editor: Caroline Smith
Managing Art Editor: Emily Cook
Photographer: Jules Selmes

ISBN 10 1-58923-185-6
ISBN 13 978-1-58923-185-6

Reproduced by RDC, Malaysia
Printed in China by Hung Hing

10 9 8 7 6 5

CONTENTS

INTRODUCTION

Ready, set, knit! In no time, you'll be making the quick and creative accessories you crave. Relaxing, creative, and stylish, knitting is a huge trend, and you'll soon know why people love it so much.

You'll be amazed at how little equipment you need to get started—just a pair of needles and a few balls of yarn. Master the first easy stitches and some simple techniques and you'll soon be able to achieve some interesting effects. From cables and lacework to colored and textured patterns, the choice is yours.

This book begins with the basics—needles and yarns, casting on and binding off, knitting and purling. It then covers those core skills you'll need to get the best results—such as getting the gauge right and increasing and decreasing. At this point, I'm sure you'll be eager to begin knitting, so I've put in some quick and easy projects to get you started.

One of the wonders of knitting is the way that it allows you to create your own textiles. By manipulating the basic knit and purl stitches, you can make patterns in your fabric that add texture and relief to your finished work. In this book, I've shown you how to achieve some of these effects, from the very subtle, such as moss stitch, to distinctly three-dimensional patterns, such as cables and bobbles. I've also shown you how to make light, lacy looking knitting by using openwork techniques.

Changing the color of the yarns as you work is another way to create patterns in your knitting. I've included the basic techniques for using color in your work as well as information on how to read a chart. There's also a feature on adding embroidery to knitting—another way to add a bit of extra color.

As you look through this book, you'll find instructions for many classic knitting patterns. Work up a few samples of these stitches to familiarize yourself with the techniques before using them in the projects.

The projects that I've designed for you use the techniques that are covered in the book, allowing you to make something that matches your skill level—so there's something for everyone. I hope you'll get as much pleasure knitting them as I did designing them. And of course you'll have the added pleasure of wearing or using something you've made yourself.

In this busy world, we shouldn't underestimate the value of traditional hand-crafts. Take up knitting and you can reclaim time for yourself to relax and unwind. You can enter a world of calm and contemplation, where day-to-day tensions and distractions slip away. Your hands and mind will work together in a natural, creative rhythm.

Knitting is a handcraft that has been passed down to us through the generations. Each generation has added new life to the craft, with new ideas, new designs and new yarns. Today, knitting is hip, colorful, and fun. Have fun with it!

EQUIPMENT AND YARNS

EQUIPMENT AND YARNS

Starting a knitting project requires little more than enthusiasm, yarn, and a pair of standard straight knitting needles. Needles are made of aluminum, plastic, wood, or bamboo and come in a range of sizes. For large pieces, and for knitting in the round, circular needles are useful, while gloves call for double-pointed needles. A few simple accessories are also helpful.

OTHER USEFUL EQUIPMENT

These help you hold or count your stitches, mark your place, or handle colors separately. Long pins and a blunt-pointed tapestry needle are needed for seams.

KNITTING NEEDLE SIZES

US	Metric (mm)
19	15.0
17	12.0
15	10.0
13	9.0
11	8.0
10½	6.5
10	6.0
9	5.5
8	5.0
7	4.5
6	4.0
5	3.75
4	3.25
3	3.0
2	2.75
1	2.25
0	2.0

TYPES OF NEEDLES

Special needles are used for cables, or for knitting in the round.

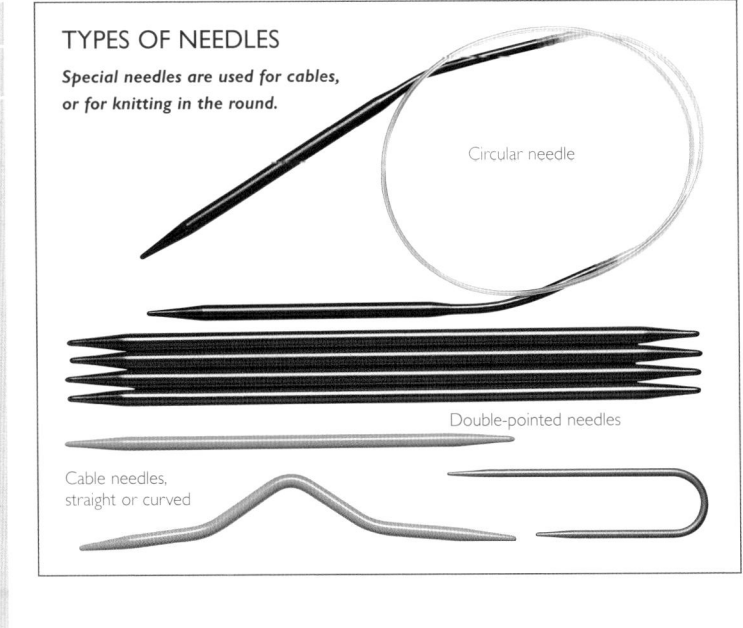

Circular needle

Double-pointed needles

Cable needles, straight or curved

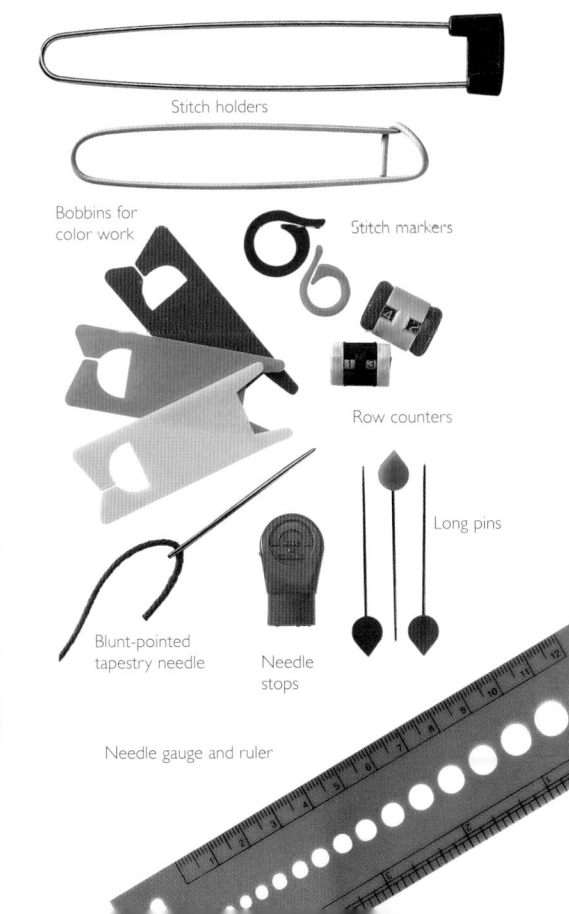

Stitch holders

Bobbins for color work

Stitch markers

Row counters

Long pins

Blunt-pointed tapestry needle

Needle stops

Needle gauge and ruler

YARN WEIGHT AND PLY

Yarns come in a range of standard weights. Knitting worsted is twice the weight of sport weight. Fisherman (Aran) is roughly equal to three strands of sport weight. Bulky is approximately equal to four strands of sport weight or two strands of knitting worsted.

The term ply refers to the number of strands which, when twisted together, make up the yarn, i.e. 2-, 3- and 4-ply are made up of that number of strands. Ply does not accurately define the weight—a thick yarn may have fewer strands than a thin one.

YARN CONTENT

Knitting yarns are made of natural or synthetic materials. Natural yarns can be of animal or vegetable fibers. The former include wool, mohair, angora, cashmere, alpaca, and silk, while vegetable fibers produce cotton or linen yarns. Synthetic yarns include polyesters and acrylics; these are easier to wash and can be worn by people sensitive to wool. Yarns are often made of blends of two different types of fiber—mohair and nylon, or wool and silk are common blends. You'll also find a wide range of novelty yarns, in varying thicknesses and textures, that can be used to create some stunning effects in your knitting.

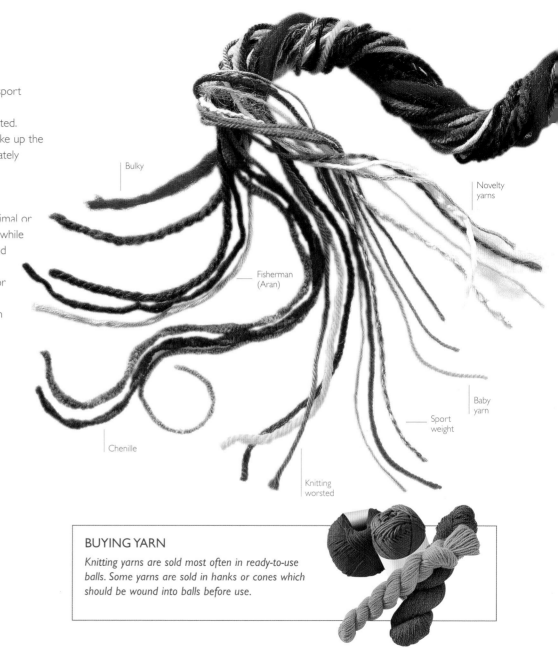

Bulky

Novelty yarns

Fisherman (Aran)

Baby yarn

Sport weight

Chenille

Knitting worsted

BUYING YARN

Knitting yarns are sold most often in ready-to-use balls. Some yarns are sold in hanks or cones which should be wound into balls before use.

CASTING ON

The first step in knitting anything is to place the required number of stitches on the needles—this is called casting on. These stitches will form one edge of the finished item, usually the bottom.

MAKING A SLIP KNOT

Make a loop and insert the needle under the short length (top). Draw the yarn through the loop and pull both ends to tighten the knot on the needle (bottom).

When you cast on to begin knitting, you want the edge to be even, so it is important that the stitches you make at this stage are all the same size. It is also necessary for these stitches to be moderately loose so that they can be worked off the needle easily as you knit the first row.

There are two methods of casting on—the one-needle cast on and the two-needle cast on. The one-needle cast-on method is probably better for beginners, as it is easy to master. However, if you find that your cast-on stitches are too snug on the needle and difficult to work, try using the two-needle cast-on method. Whichever method you choose, make a slip knot before you begin to form the first stitch.

ONE-NEEDLE CAST-ON EDGE

You start this method at a measured distance from the end of the yarn. Allow 1 inch (2.5 cm) per stitch for heavyweight yarn and ½ inch (1.25 cm) per stitch for lightweight. For example, to cast on 24 stitches in knitting worsted, make a slip knot 24 inches (60 cm) plus 6 inches (15 cm) from the yarn end. (You need an allowance of about 6 inches [15 cm] at the end of the yarn.) The cast-on stitches will form a firm, yet elastic, foundation for all subsequent stitches, which is suitable for all patterns except those with a delicate edge.

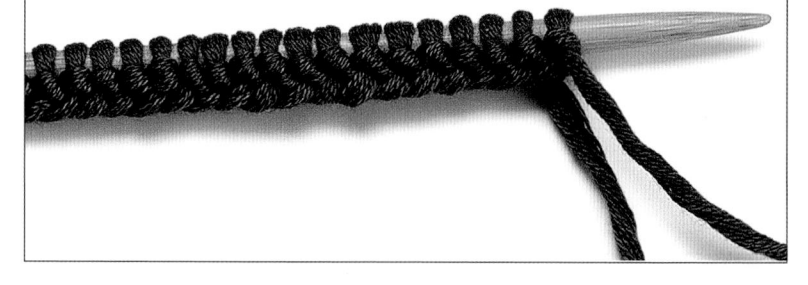

TWO-NEEDLE CAST-ON EDGE

With this method, each new stitch is formed as a knit stitch (see page 11) and transferred to the left needle. If you work through the loop fronts on the first row of knitting, it produces a soft, loose edge, suitable for fine lace stitches. If you work through the loop backs on the first row, a firmer edge will be produced. Casting on with this method is useful when increasing stitches at one side or when completing a buttonhole.

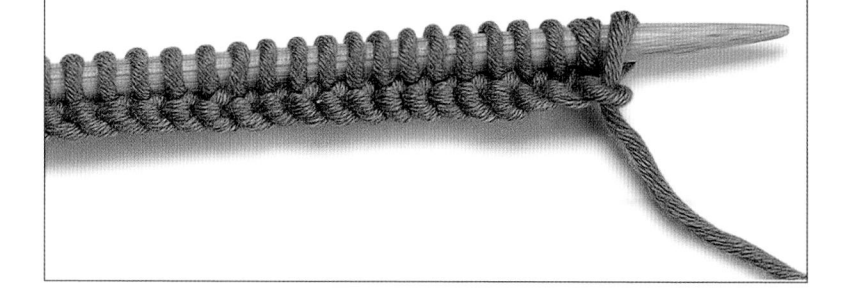

ONE-NEEDLE CAST ON

1. Allowing sufficient yarn for the number of stitches you want to cast on plus 6 inches (15 cm) extra, make a slip knot; hold the needle in your right hand. Hold the strands of yarn securely between the ring and little fingers of your left hand.

2. Slip your left forefinger and thumb between the strands so that the strand from the skein is at the back, and the working yarn is at the front.

3. Bring your left thumb up and spread your other fingers, still holding onto the yarn ends with your ring and little fingers.

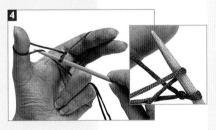

4. Take the needle under the yarn held across your thumb (left) and then up to the yarn on your left forefinger (right).

5. Putting the point of the needle behind the yarn on your left forefinger (left), draw the needle and yarn through the loop on your thumb to make the stitch (right). Let the loop slip from your thumb and pull both ends to secure the new stitch. Repeat steps 1 to 5 for each required stitch.

TWO-NEEDLE CAST ON

1. Make a slip knot about 6 inches (15 cm) from the yarn end and hold the needle in your left hand. Insert your right-hand needle through the front of the loop and under the left-hand needle. Pass the working yarn under and over its tip.

2. With your right-hand needle, draw the yarn through the slip knot to form a stitch.

3. Transfer the new stitch to your left-hand needle, placing it next to the slip knot. Insert your right-hand needle through the front of the new stitch and under the left-hand needle. Pass the working yarn under and over its tip to make the next new stitch. Continue in this way to cast on the required number of stitches.

LEFT-HANDED KNITTERS

Reverse the instructions for left and right hands if you are left handed. To cast on using the one-needle method, hold the needle in your left hand and manipulate the working yarn with your right hand. When knitting and when casting on with the two-needle method, hold the needle carrying the stitches in your right hand and insert the left needle through the stitches. If you like, place this book in front of a mirror to follow the correct hand positions.

KNIT STITCH

The knit stitch (along with the purl stitch, see pages 12–13), is often called plain knitting. Using just a knit stitch, you can create a wide range of garments or decor items. The knit stitch forms a flat, vertical loop on the fabric face. The simplest fabric is created by knitting every row, which is known as garter stitch; this makes two identical ridged and furrowed sides. Endless pattern combinations can be produced by using the knit stitch and the purl stitch.

SOFT EDGE
Knit through the front of the stitch on the first row.

FIRM EDGE
Knit through the back of the stitch, crossing the yarn.

❖ GARTER STITCH

This stitch is most commonly formed by knitting every row, but the same effect is achieved by purling every row. The work formed stays flat and firm, resists curling, and is good for borders, buttonhole bands, and edgings. It has a loose structure with "give" in both directions.

ENGLISH

In this method, use your right hand to draw the yarn around the right needle. The amount of yarn released with each stitch is controlled by wrapping the working yarn between your two end fingers. Your left hand propels the knitting forward while your right hand makes the stitch—raising the thread, placing it over the needle, and pulling it through the loop.

1. *Hold the needle with cast-on stitches in your left hand. Take yarn around the little finger of your right hand, under the next two fingers, and over the top of your forefinger.*

2. *Keeping the yarn behind the work, hold the second needle in your right hand and insert it into the front of the first stitch.*

3. *With your right forefinger, take the yarn forward under and over the point of the right needle.*

4. *Draw the yarn through the loop and push the resulting stitch toward the tip of the left needle so you can slip it onto your right needle.*

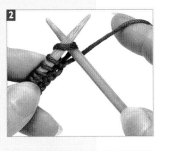

CONTINENTAL

In this method, often found to be faster than holding yarn in your right hand, you use the forefinger of your left hand to keep the yarn under tension and to scoop the yarn onto the right needle. The amount of yarn released is controlled partly by your last two fingers, and partly by your forefinger. Hold your left hand up slightly to help keep the yarn taut.

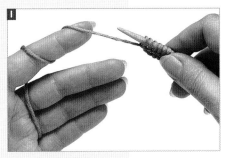

1. *Hold the needle with the cast-on stitches in your right hand. Wrap the yarn over your left forefinger, let it fall across the palm and take up the slack between the last two fingers.*

2. *With the work in your left hand, extend your forefinger, pulling the yarn behind the needle. Using your thumb and middle finger, push the first stitch toward the tip and insert the right needle into the front of the stitch.*

3. *Twist the right needle and pull the tip under the working yarn to draw the loop onto the right needle.*

4. *If necessary, hold the loop with your right forefinger while you pull it down through the stitch. Pull the new stitch onto the right needle.*

PURL STITCH

PURL STITCH

Along with the knit stitch, the purl stitch is the other fundamental stitch. When one row is knitted and the other purled, they form stockinette stitch, which has a smooth knitted side and a pebbly purled one. If used on its own, purl stitch also produces garter stitch.

❖ STOCKINETTE STITCH

This basic and versatile knitting pattern is formed by working one row in knit and the next in purl. It produces work that tends to curl if not blocked (see page 26). It stretches more widthwise than from top to bottom. The knit side is generally used as the right side.

❖ REVERSE STOCKINETTE STITCH

This is knitted in the same way as stockinette stitch, but with the purl side used as the right side. It is often used as a background for cables and other raised patterns.

ENGLISH

The movements here are opposite those for knit stitch. The needle is put into the front of the stitch, then the yarn, which is held in the front, is thrown over the back of the needle. Purl stitches tend to be looser than knit ones, so keep your forefinger closer to the work to help make the stitches even.

1 *Hold the needle with stitches (cast-on or knit) in your left hand. Wrap yarn around your little finger, under your next two fingers, and over the forefinger of your right hand.*

2 *Keeping the yarn in front of the work, pick up the needle in your right hand and insert the point into the front of the first stitch on the left needle.*

3 *With your right forefinger, take the yarn over the point of the right needle, and then under it.*

4 *Draw the loop on the right needle through the stitch and push the new stitch toward the tip of the left needle so you can slip it onto your right needle.*

CONTINENTAL

With this method, your left forefinger holds the working yarn taut while you scoop up a new loop with your right needle. This action is helped by twisting your left wrist forward to release the yarn and using your middle finger to push the yarn toward the tip of the needle.

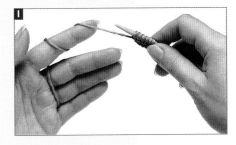

1 *Hold the needle with the stitches in your right hand. Wrap the yarn over your left forefinger, let it fall across your palm, and take up the slack between your last two fingers.*

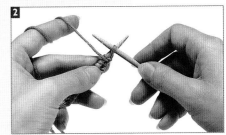

2 *With the work in your left hand, extend your forefinger slightly, pulling the working yarn in front of the needle. With your thumb and middle finger, push the first stitch toward the tip and insert the right needle into the front of the stitch. Hold the stitch with your right forefinger.*

3 *Twisting your left wrist back slightly, use the forefinger of your left hand to wrap the yarn around the right needle.*

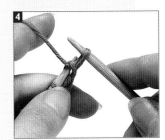

4 *Push down and back with the right needle to draw the loop through the stitch and slip the new stitch onto the right needle. Straighten your left forefinger to tighten the new stitch.*

SLIP-STITCH SELVAGE (*left*)
On all right sides of work (knit rows): Slip the first stitch knitwise then knit the last stitch. On all wrong sides of work (purl rows): Slip the first stitch purlwise then purl the last stitch.

GARTER-STITCH SELVAGE (*below*)
Knit the right-side rows as usual, and knit the first and last stitches of every wrong-side (purl) row.

BINDING OFF

This technique provides a finished edge at the end of your work and is also used to shape arm- and buttonholes. Usually you bind off on the right side of the work, knitting knit stitches and purling purl stitches. It is important that you bind off somewhat loosely, otherwise the edge may pull in and become distorted. If your stitches are too tight, try casting off with a needle one size larger than used for the work, or use the suspended cast off method.

DOUBLE GARTER-STITCH BORDER (*left*)
On every row: Slip the first stitch knitwise and knit the second stitch; knit the last two stitches.

DOUBLE CHAIN BORDER (*below*)
On all right sides of work (knit rows): Slip the first stitch knitwise, purl the second stitch. Knit to the last two stitches, then purl one and slip last stitch knitwise.

SELVAGES

The cast-on and bound-off stitches usually form the top and bottom ends of the work, and often have another finish applied to them, such as a fringe or neckband. The sides, known as selvages, may be sewn into a seam or left exposed. If the sides are to be joined, use one of the simple selvage edges since they are easier to sew. If you are knitting something with exposed edges, such as a scarf or blanket, use a border. This will be more attractive and help the finished piece lie flat.

SIMPLE VARIATIONS

A stockinette edge is formed by alternate knit and purl rows. Beginning knitters often have trouble keeping this edge tight. By slightly varying your technique, you can create a more stable edge and one more suitable for seams. Slip-stitch selvage is recommended with edge-to-edge seams; garter-stitch selvage is effective for backstitched and oversewn seams.

BORDERS

If you want a special edge on your work, you may have to add two additional stitches on each side. The double garter-stitch edge is firm and even, and will not curl. The double chain edge is also firm but more decorative.

PLAIN METHOD

This produces a firm, plain edge that is suitable for seaming and armhole and buttonhole shaping.

1 *Work your first two stitches in pattern. *Keeping the yarn at the back, insert the tip of your left-hand needle through the first stitch.*

2 *Lift the first stitch over the second stitch and off your needle.*

3 *Work the next stitch in pattern.* Repeat sequence set out between the asterisks until the desired number of stitches are bound off. Secure yarn at end (see box below).*

SUSPENDED METHOD

More flexible than the plain bind off, this method produces a looser edge and is preferable if your selvages tend to be tight.

1 *Work the first two stitches in pattern. *Keeping yarn at the back, insert the tip of your left needle through the first stitch. Lift the first stitch over the second stitch off the right needle, and retain on left needle.*

2 *Work the next stitch and drop the held stitch when you complete a new stitch.**

3 *Repeat the instructions between the asterisks until two stitches are left. Knit these two together. Secure the yarn at the end (see box below).*

SECURING THE YARN END

After binding off with either of the two methods above, you will have a single stitch left on your needle. Slip this off your needle, take the yarn end and slip it through the last stitch and pull firmly to tighten the loop. Then, using a tapestry needle, weave the secured yarn end into the seam edge to a depth of 2 to 3 inches (5–7.5 cm).

STITCH GAUGE

STITCH GAUGE

At the beginning of every knitting pattern you will find the stitch gauge—the number of stitches and rows you should end up with for a given measure when using the specified needles and yarn.

This measure is very important to the size and fit of a garment. Before beginning a new project, make a sample swatch of approximately 4 inches (10 cm) to check that you will get the desired results using the number of stitches and rows over a given measure as set out in the pattern.

CHECKING YOUR GAUGE

Using the given tension as a guide, and the needles and yarn designated, cast on four times the number of stitches that equals **1** inch (2.5 cm). Then take your sample and pin it to a flat surface; do not stretch it. Use a ruler, plastic tape measure, or stitch gauge to measure both horizontally and vertically.

MAKING ADJUSTMENTS

If your stitch gauge does not exactly equal that given, change needle size and knit another sample. One needle size makes a difference of about one stitch over 2 inches (5 cm). If you have more stitches to the inch, your tension is too tight and you should change to larger needles. If you have fewer stitches, your tension is too loose so use smaller needles.

THE EFFECT OF YARNS AND PATTERNS

Yarn and pattern also affect tension, so it is especially important to make a sample if you are changing either one from that called for in the instructions. Loosely spun or thick yarns, such as knitting worsted or novelty yarn, will knit up with many fewer stitches and rows than firmly spun yarns, such as silk. Rib and other textured patterns produce much tighter work than do lacy patterns.

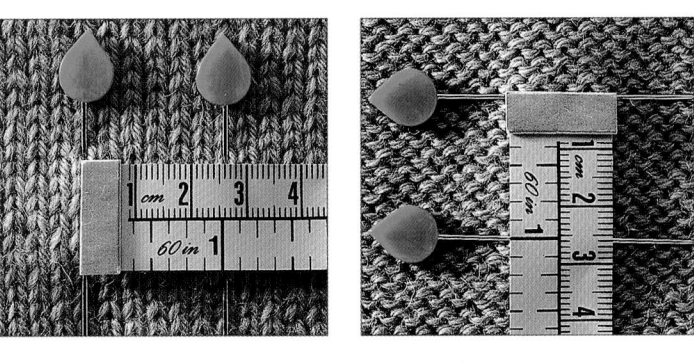

HORIZONTAL MEASURE

In stockinette, it is easier to measure on the knit side, where each loop represents one stitch. In garter stitch, count the loops in one row only. Place two pins 1 inch (2.5 cm) apart and count the stitches between them.

VERTICAL MEASURE

In stockinette, it is easier to measure on the purl side (two ridges are one row). In garter stitch, a ridge is one row and a valley another. Place two pins 1 inch (2.5 cm) apart and count the number of rows between them.

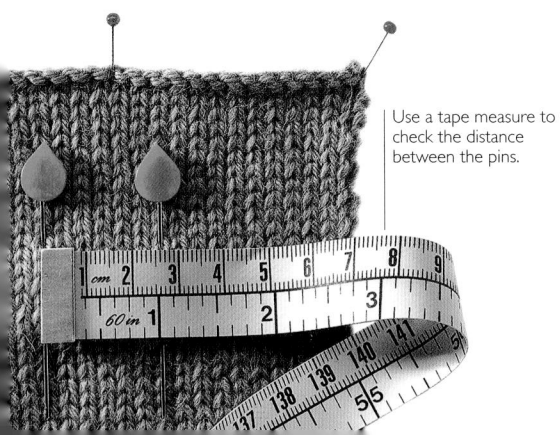

Use a tape measure to check the distance between the pins.

Sport weight is the finest of the three yarns and produces the smallest square.

Knitting worsted, worked to the same number of stitches, makes a larger piece than sport weight.

Fisherman's (Aran) yarn is the bulkiest yarn of the three and has fewest stitches to the inch.

CORRECTING MISTAKES

The sooner you notice an error the easier it is to correct. If a stitch has fallen off the needle one row down, retrieve it using your knitting needles. If you don't, it will form a run, and you will need a crochet hook to pick it up.

RAVELING YOUR WORK

Mark the row where your error is. Take the work off the needles and carefully pull the working yarn, until you are one row above the error. To replace stitches on needle, hold yarn at back, and insert your left needle into front row of first stitch below unpicked row. Pull on working yarn to remove top stitch.

To correct a run of dropped stitches, have the knit side of the work facing you. Insert the crochet hook into the front of the fallen stitch and pick up the loose yarn behind. Draw the yarn through the stitch, forming a new stitch. Continue until you reach the top of the run.

If you knit a stitch incorrectly one or two rows down, unpick it and then correct it in the same way. If a mistake has occurred near the start of your piece, you will have to ravel your work to get close to it. If you are working in stockinette or ribbing, always pick up stitches with the knit side toward you, as this is easiest. Be careful not to twist any of the stitches.

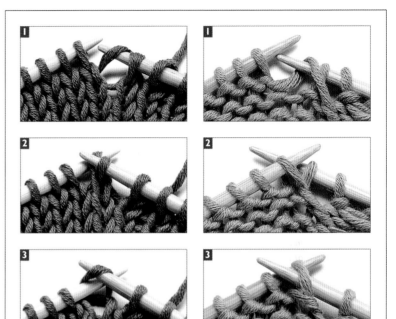

RETRIEVING A DROPPED KNIT STITCH

Insert your right needle into the front of the dropped stitch, picking up the loose yarn behind it [1]. Take your left needle into the back of the stitch and gently lift the stitch up and over the loose yarn and off the right needle [2]. To transfer the new stitch, insert the left needle into the front so that the stitch slips onto it in the correct working position [3].

RETRIEVING A DROPPED PURL STITCH

Insert your right needle into the back of the dropped stitch, picking up the loose yarn in front [1]. Take your left needle into the front of the stitch and gently lift the stitch up and over the loose yarn and off the needle [2]. Insert the left needle into the new stitch on the right needle and slip the new stitch onto it in the correct working position [3].

KNITTING TERMS

A set of standard abbreviations, terms, and symbols have been devised in order to reduce knitting instructions to their shortest possible length.

WHY USE ABBREVIATIONS?

To illustrate why abbreviations make such a big difference when writing out patterns here is an example of a simple pattern (for moss stitch rib) written out in full:
On the first row, knit 5 stitches. Knit 1 stitch and purl 1 stitch three times and then knit 5 stitches. Repeat this last bit until you get to the end of the row.
On the second row, purl 5 stitches and then purl 1 stitch and knit 1 stitch three times. Repeat this last bit until there are 5 stitches left on the needle and then purl the remaining stitches.

It's easier and clearer to write:
Row 1: K5, *[k1, p1] 3 times, k5; rep from * to end.
Row 2: *P5, [p1, k1] 3 times; rep from * to last 5 sts, p5.

If you were to write out the instructions for a knitting pattern in full it would run to several pages, even for the simplest of garments. That is why a range of abbreviations and special terms have come to be used in knitting patterns to keep them as short as possible. Many patterns repeat elements across a row and from row to row. Rather than write out each repeat every time it appears, there are commonly used terms and devices that help keep the written instructions short and easy to follow.

Most patterns will give you an explanation of the terms and symbols used but you'll find that most abbreviations are the same, whatever the pattern, and that over time you will come to recognize them instantly.

REPEATS

Because a knitting pattern usually consists of sequences of stitches, two devices are used to express this in the shortest possible space. One is the asterisk*, which is placed before the instruction it relates to. For example, P2, *k2, p2; rep from *, end k2, means you purl the first two stitches, then for the rest of the row until you are two stitches from the end, you knit two, purl two. The last two stitches are knitted. Brackets are also used to indicate repeats. For example, P2 [k2, p2] ten times, k3 means that after purling your first two stitches you repeat the sequence of knitting two and purling two ten times (a total of 40 stitches) before knitting the last three.

MULTIPLES

Preceding the stitch sample patterns in this book is an instruction about the number of stitches required to complete the pattern across the row. This is expressed as a multiple of a number of stitches, for example, multiple of 6 sts. It may also include an additional number to balance the pattern or account for a diagonal, for example, multiple of 6 sts plus 3. The number of stitches on the needle must be divisible by the multiple, so for a multiple of 5 sts plus 2, you would need to cast on 5 + 2, 10 + 2, 15 + 2,.... 100 + 2, etc. In the pattern instructions, the multiple is expressed in the following ways:

Multiple of 8 sts plus 2
Row 1: *K4, p4*, k2
Row 2: *P4, k4*, p2
or
Row 1: *K4, p4, rep from *, end k2
Row 2: *P4, k4, rep from *, end p2

alt	alternate
beg	beginning
CC	contrasting color
cn	cable needle
dec(s)	decrease(s), (see page 23)
dpn	double-pointed needle(s)
k	knit
k1b	knit into the back of the stitch
k2tog	knit 2 stitches together
k2tog tbl	knit 2 stitches together through the back of both loops
k-wise	insert needle as though to knit
inc(s)	increase(s), (see page 21)
lp	loop
M1	make 1, (see page 21)
MC	main color
p	purl
patt	pattern
psso	pass slipped stitch over the knitted one, (see page 23)
p2tog	purl 2 stitches together
p2tog tbl	purl 2 stitches together through the back of both loops
p-wise	insert needle as though to purl
RS	right side(s)
rem	remaining
rep	repeat
rnd(s)	rounds
sk	skip
sl	slip (always slip stitches purlwise unless otherwise instructed)
sl st	slip stitch, (see page 23)
ssk	slip, slip, knit decrease (see page 89)
st(s)	stitch(es)
st st	stockinette stitch
tbl	through back of loop (work into back of stitch)
tog	together
WS	wrong side(s)
yb	yarn behind
yf	yarn forward
yo	yarn over needle, (see page 87)
*	Work instructions immediately following *, then repeat as directed, (see Repeats, page 18)
[ ]	Work or repeat all instructions enclosed in brackets as directed immediately after, (see Repeats, page 18)
—	The number of sts that should be on your needles or across a row is given after a dash at the end of the row. This serves as a check point, especially after a section of increasing or decreasing.

INCREASING

When you are knitting a garment that requires shaping, you will need to add stitches, which is called increasing. This technique is also necessary when you are creating certain stitch patterns, such as bobbles (see page 51), and openwork patterns (see pages 86–91).

Where increases are made in garment shaping, they are often worked in pairs so that the item widens equally on both sides. Where increases are made in decorative stitch patterns, they are combined with decreases (see pages 22–23) so the total number of stitches remains constant.

There are several methods of producing increases. The yarn-over method (see page 87) is visible and is used for openwork patterns. The other methods are called invisible. In reality, all increases can be seen but some are more obvious than others and different methods are used at different times.

The bar and make-one increases shown here are all invisible increases, and are typically used in garment shaping. When you are creating a gradual shape, such as a sleeve, it is neater to make the increases two or three stitches in from the sides and to use one of the invisible increases. With a complicated pattern, you will find it easier to add the stitches at the edges.

DOUBLE AND MULTIPLE INCREASES

To make two increases in the same stitch (M2), knit, purl, and knit into the front of the stitch. To make more than two stitches, as in bobble and embossed patterns (see page 51), continue to knit and purl in the same stitch for the number of stitches that must be made. An increase of, say, five stitches is used to form a large bobble.

These warm woolly hats use shaping techniques to make them snug and to create the ear flaps (see pages 46–47).

BAR METHOD

This frequently used technique produces a small horizontal stitch on the right side of the work, hence its name. It is commonly abbreviated as *Inc 1*. You knit (or purl) into the front and back of a stitch to make two stitches. This type of increase can be used near the edge of the work when shaping garments or when making bobbles, where the "bump" will not matter.

1. *Knit a stitch in the usual way but do not remove it from your left-hand needle.*

2. *Insert your right-hand needle into back of the same stitch and knit again.*

3. *Remove the stitch from your needle. The extra stitch formed by this method produces a small bump on the right side. This will not be noticeable at the edge of the work.*

MAKE ONE

Here, you pick up the horizontal strand between two stitches and knit (or purl) into it to make a new stitch. To make it virtually invisible, you have to work into the back of the strand so that it twists. It is effective for shaping darts on mitten or glove thumbs, and is commonly abbreviated as *M1*.

1. *Insert your left-hand needle from front to back under the horizontal strand between two stitches.*

2. *Knit (or purl) into the back of the strand on your left-hand needle.*

3. *Transfer the stitch onto your right-hand needle; the twist in the stitch prevents a gap from appearing.*

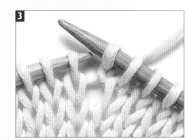

DECREASING

When shaping knitted items and creating stitch patterns, decreasing the number of stitches on your needles is as important as increasing for achieving the desired effects.

When you are knitting, you sometimes have to lose several stitches along one row, for example, when shaping an armhole or neckline. Binding off (pages 14–15) is the preferred method of decreasing when three or more stitches have to be lost. However, if only one or two stitches have to be decreased, any of the methods described on page 23 could be used. Each method is visible on the right side of the work and will pull the stitches on a diagonal, either to the right or the left. If you are decreasing randomly, or at the edge of the work, the direction of the slant is not important.

PAIRED DECREASES

In symmetrical shaping, however, such as with a raglan sleeve or V-neck opening, the decreases must be paired, to the right and left of the center. In other words, if the decrease to the right of the center slants left, the decrease to

the left of the center must slant right. Right slants are made by knitting (or purling) two stitches together through the front of both loops; left slants are made by working through the back of both loops.

Slip-stitch decreases slant in only one direction, from right to left in knit stitch and from left to right in purl. So in the same row they are generally used in combination with knitting two stitches together.

Binding off is used to decrease stitches and shape the armholes and shoulders of this funky fringed top (see pages 28–29).

KNITTING TWO STITCHES TOGETHER

Decreasing by knitting two stitches together creates a slightly tighter decrease than the slip-stitch method. It is abbreviated *k2tog* for a right slant, *k2tog tbl* for a left slant. A slant to the right is used at the left edge of the work, a slant to the left, at the right edge.

RIGHT SLANT

1. *To make a right slant (k2tog): Insert your needle in the next two stitches through the front of both loops. Take the yarn around the needle and draw it through.*

2. *Transfer the new stitch to your right-hand needle.*

LEFT SLANT

1. *To make a left slant (k2tog tbl): Insert your needle in the next two stitches through the back of both loops. Take the yarn around the needle.*

2. *Draw the thread through and transfer the new stitch to your right-hand needle.*

THE SLIP-STITCH DECREASE

This results in a slightly looser decrease than knitting two stitches together. When made on a knit row, it slants from right to left, and is abbreviated *Sl 1, k1, psso*. A similar decrease can be made on a purl row, when it slants from left to right. It is abbreviated *Sl 1, p1, psso*.

ON A KNIT ROW

1. *Slip one stitch knitwise from your left-hand needle onto the right needle then knit the next stitch.*

2. *Insert your left-hand needle into the front of the slipped stitch and pull it over the knitted one.*

3. *The right-to-left slant made by this decrease in a knit row is used on the right side of the center of the work.*

PURL METHODS

You can purl two stitches together. Purling through the front of both loops (p2tog) gives a right slant. Purling through the back of both loops (p2togtbl) gives a left slant.

To use a slip-stitch decrease on a purl row, slip a stitch purlwise onto your right-hand needle and then purl the next stitch before pulling the slipped stitch over.

CHUNKY SCARF

A brightly colored, bulky wool yarn has been used to knit this simple yet appealing scarf. Knitted entirely with garter stitch on large needles, this is a great first project and a chance to enjoy knitting with an exciting novelty yarn.

❖ SIZES
43" x 8" (109 x 20 cm)

❖ MATERIALS
Yarn Bulky novelty yarn 100% wool (approx 54 yds/50 m per 100 g). 3 x 100 g balls
Needles One pair No. 17 (12 mm) or size to obtain gauge
Notions Crochet hook

❖ GAUGE
8 sts and 10 rows = 4" (10 cm) in garter st.

❖ SKILLS USED
Garter st (p10), slip-stitch selvage (p14)

See pages 18–19 for knitting terms.

MINI BAG

This pretty, petite garter stitch bag is knitted in washable cotton yarn. Simply knit it flat and then fold it and seam the sides. The angled flap is shaped by decreasing until the stitches are gone.

❖ SIZES
6" x 7½" (10 x 19 cm)

❖ MATERIALS
Yarn Sport weight 100% cotton (approx 126 yds/115 m per 50 g). 2 x 50 g balls
Needles One pair No. 5 (3.75 mm) or size to obtain gauge
Notions Tapestry needle, button

❖ GAUGE
22 sts and 42 rows = 4" (10 cm) in garter st.

❖ SKILLS USED
Garter st (p10), decreasing (p22), seams (p27), twisted cord (p69)

See pages 18–19 for knitting terms.

CHUNKY SCARF

Use a slip-stitch selvage (see page 14) to give a firm edge.

Using bulky wool and No. 17 needles, cast on 16 sts and work in garter st (see page 10) until piece measures 43" (109 cm). Cut several 10" (25 cm) lengths of yarn and, using a crochet hook, knot along the cast off and bound off edges to make fringe (see page 35). Steam gently.

CHANGING TO A NEW YARN

When you've finished one ball of yarn and want to change to a new one, it's best to do this at the beginning of a new row, rather than in the middle. You can use the same technique that you would use to change to a new color; see page 61.

MINI BAG
BACK AND FRONT

Using sport weight cotton and No. 5 needles, cast on 34 sts and work in garter st (see page 10) until piece measures 16" (40.5 cm).

SHAPE FLAP

K2 tog at beg and end of each row until 2 sts remain. Bind off.

FINISHING

With RS facing, fold piece 7½" (19 cm) up from cast-on edge to make body of bag. Thread a tapestry needle with some yarn and stitch the side edges together (see page 27). Turn to RS, fold bag flap over.

MAKE LOOP FOR BUTTON

Cast on 20 sts. Bind off. Fold loop in half and sew onto point on bound-off edge of bag on inside.

Attach button directly beneath loop on front of bag. Make a 38" (96.5 cm) twisted cord with tassel ends (see page 69) and stitch to the sides of bag. Steam lightly.

BLOCKING AND PRESSING

Before a knitted garment is sewn together, all of its pieces must be shaped to the measurements given in the pattern and then ironed. The process smoothes out any irregular stitches and flattens curling edges.

PRESSING

After pinning cotton and wool knitting, press it very lightly under a damp cloth with a warm iron. Alternatively, hold a steaming iron very close to, but not touching, the knitting. Leave until completely dry. For synthetic yarn, check label instructions. The beauty of the garment is in its hand-knitted appearance—be careful not to over-press and destroy this look.

BLOCKING

You will need a large, flat, padded surface. A table covered with a folded blanket and topped with a clean white sheet works well. Before you begin, weave in any loose ends. Then place each knitted piece wrong side up on the padding, smooth it out, and pin the corners to the padding with straight steel pins. Take care not to stretch or distort the basic shape, and make sure the knit rows run in straight lines. Then take a tape measure and check the length and width of each piece against those given in the pattern. Stretch or shrink the piece as necessary, and continue pinning at fairly close intervals all around the edges. The edges should be quite smooth: if each pin draws out a point of the knitting, you are either stretching it too much or are not using enough pins.

Use minimum pinning on ribbed garments or on those parts of garments that contain ribbing. The ribbing should not be under any tension. Steam ribbing, don't press it.

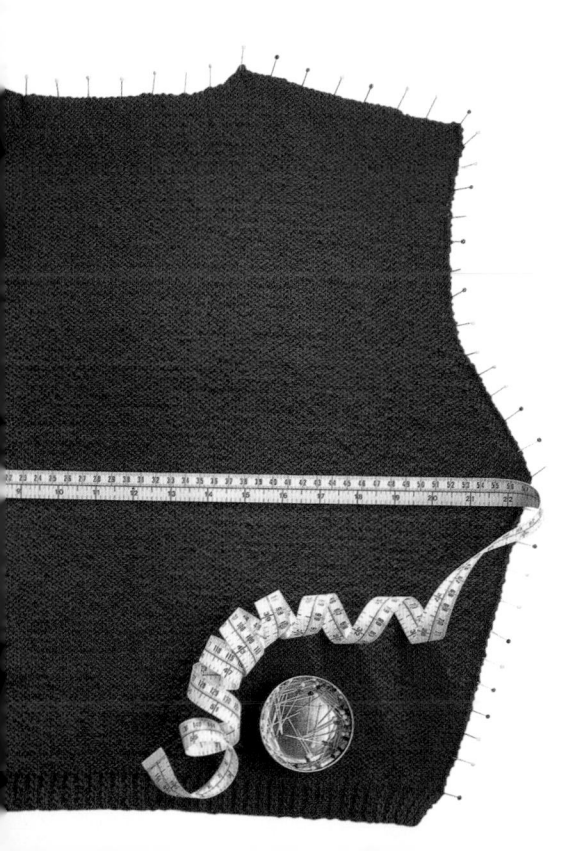

STOCKINETTE AND GARTER STITCH

Press or steam each part of the knitting. If pressing, lift up and re-apply the iron rather than moving it over the surface of the cloth as this will distort the stitches.

EMBOSSED PATTERNS

Hold a steaming iron or steamer just above the knitting. If you press, use a damp cloth and unpin the piece immediately and lightly pat it into shape so that the texture isn't flattened.

SEAMS

Once you've finished knitting all the pieces of

a garment, you need to sew them together.

Don't be tempted to rush this process because clumsy seaming can completely ruin beautiful knitting. Seams should be sewn with a blunt-ended tapestry needle and matching yarn. If the garment yarn is not smooth, use plain yarn in a matching or slightly darker color, making sure the washing instructions are compatible. A ladder-stitch seam is best for straight edges, and can be almost invisible. Backstitch seams will make a small ridge inside the garment. If you are joining two pieces of horizontal knitting when the stitches are not bound off first, use the grafting method.

LADDER-STITCH SEAM

Place the pieces edge to edge, with right sides facing up. Match the knitting row by row. With your needle pick up the strand between the 1st and 2nd stitches on one edge, and then the strand between the 1st and 2nd stitches on the other edge. Take care to match the tension of the knitting.

GRAFTING OR KITCHENER STITCH

Slip the stitches off the needles. To prevent your work from raveling, press lightly or thread a length of yarn through the stitches. Place the pieces face up on a padded surface, with edges to be joined abutting. Thread a tapestry needle with matching yarn. Insert the needle from back to front through the first loop on the lower piece. *Insert the needle from front to back through the first loop on the upper piece; then from back to front on the second upper loop. Insert the needle from front to back in the first lower loop, then from back to front in the second lower loop. Repeat from *, always going from front to back through a loop you have already gone through from back to front. If worried about knitting running, keep work on needles, slipping off two at a time as you graft.

BACKSTITCH SEAM

Place the pieces right sides together, matching the rows of knitting stitch for stitch. Baste together with a contrasting yarn. Backstitch along the seam, ¼ inch (6 mm) in, sewing into the center of each stitch and checking the stitches correspond on both pieces. To work backstitch: bring the needle one stitch ahead at the starting edge, insert it one stitch back and bring it out one stitch ahead of the emerging thread. Repeat to the end and remove the basting thread.

TO SET IN SLEEVES

The sleeve cap is often slightly larger than the armhole. The following steps will ensure a good fit. Fold the sleeve in half lengthways and mark the center cap. Match it to the shoulder seam on the garment and pin in position. Then pin the pieces together at intervals, easing in the sleeve fullness. Sew the sleeve into the armhole.

FRINGED TOP

Oh-so-easy to make and very effective on the dance floor!

This top requires just two types of yarn and knits up very quickly.

For an even simpler effect, you can omit the tied-on fringe and

increase the overall length.

❖ **SIZES**
XS, S, M, L, XL: To fit bust 32 (34, 36, 38, 40)" (81 [86,
91.5, 96.5, 101.5] cm). Finished size: 33 (35, 37, 40, 42)"
(84[89, 94, 99, 104] cm)

❖ **MATERIALS**
Yarn Extra Super Bulky 100% merino wool (approx 33
yds/30 m per 100 g). 2(2, 2, 2, 2) x 100 g balls Color A.
2(2, 3, 3, 3) x 100 g balls Color B
Needles One pair No. 19 (15 mm) or size to
obtain gauge
Notions Tapestry needle, stitch holder, crochet hook

❖ **GAUGE**
5½ sts and 8 rows = 4" (10 cm) over
stockinette stitch

❖ **SKILLS USED**
Stockinette st (p12), decreasing (p22),
seams (p27), changing color (p60)

See pages 18–19 for knitting terms.

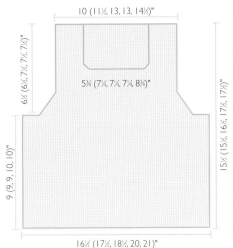

10 (11½, 13, 13, 14½)"

6½ (6½, 7¼, 7¼, 7½)"

5¾ (7¼, 7¼, 7¼, 8¾)"

15½ (15½, 16¼, 17½, 17½)"

9 (9, 9, 10, 10)"

16½ (17½, 18½, 20, 21)"

FRINGED TOP
BACK

Using Color A, cast on 22 (24, 26, 28, 30) sts. Using st st throughout, work 14 (14, 14, 15, 15) rows.
With Color B work 4 (4, 4, 5, 5) rows.

SHAPE ARMHOLES

Bind off 2 sts at beg of next 2 rows—18 (20, 22, 24, 26) sts.
Dec 1 st at both ends of next 2 (2, 2, 3, 3) rows—14 (16, 18, 18, 20) sts. Continue even until armhole measures 6½ (6½, 7½, 7½, 7½)" (16.5 [16.5, 19, 19, 19] cm) ending on WS row.

SHAPE SHOULDERS

Bind off 3 (3, 4, 4, 4) sts at beg of next 2 rows. Bind off remaining 8 (10, 10, 10, 12) sts.

FRONT

Work as for back until front is 6 (6, 8, 8, 8) rows less than back ending on a WS row.

NECK SHAPING

K4 (4, 5, 5, 5) sts, bind off 6 (8, 8, 8, 10) sts. K4 (4, 5, 5, 5) sts.

Turn and working on last 4 (4, 5, 5, 5) sts, purl to last 2 sts, p2tog—3 (3, 4, 4, 4) sts.
Work 4 (4, 6, 6, 6) rows st st. Bind off.
With 4 (4, 5, 5, 5) sts left on needle and WS facing, start using a new length of yarn and p2 tog, p to end of row.
Work 4 (4, 6, 6, 6) rows st st. Bind off.

FINISHING

Join shoulder and side seams.
Cut 16" (41 cm) lengths of Color B, thread through cast-on edge of sweater at regular intervals and attach with crochet hook every 2" (5 cm) to make fringe (see page 35).

TAKING MEASUREMENTS

Accurate measurements will ensure a better fit, no matter the pattern. Compare your measurements with those given in a pattern and your stitch gauge sample (see page 16) to check what adjustments you'll have to make. Most patterns give a body measurement, and a finished measurement of the knitted garment, which allows for ease of fit. Make sure you measure over your underclothes. The basic body measurements include the following but you may not need them all: Armhole [a], shoulder length [b], bust or chest [c], waist [d], hips [e], sleeve [f], outer arm [g], wrist [h], and shoulder width [i].

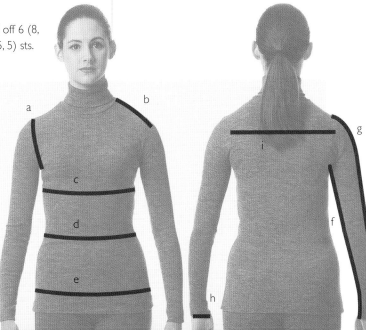

TEXTURED PATTERNS

With only the two basic stitches, a wide variety of patterns can be created.

Though the techniques are simple, the results are often sophisticated.

Textured patterns lend themselves to a wide variety of garments.

In combination, the two basic stitches, knit and purl, accentuate each other, creating texture. When they are worked vertically, the knit rows tend to stand out from the purl ones. When they are worked horizontally, in welt or ridge patterns, the purl rows stand away from the knit rows. In textured patterns, the stitches form subtle designs that alter the surface of the fabric.

Vertical rows of knit and purl are known as ribbing, and will stretch in a crosswise direction. This quality is ideal for use on garment edges, and for children's clothes because the garment will expand to accommodate the growing child. Working into the back of the knit stitches (twisted rib) helps the rib keep its shape. To be sure cuffs and waistbands are snug fitting, use smaller needles than those used for the body of the garment.

Even simple ribbing can create pattern and interest, as on these hats (see page 36). A more complex basketweave pattern adds texture to this hooded sweater (see page 82).

BROKEN RIB

Multiple of 2 sts plus 1

Row 1 (right side): K.

Row 2: P1, *k1, p1; rep from * to end.

Rows 1 to 2 form the pattern.

DOUBLE MOSS STITCH

Multiple of 4 sts plus 2

Row 1: K2, *p2, k2; rep from * to end.

Row 2: P2, *k2, p2; rep from * to end.

Row 3: As row 2.

Row 4: As row 1.

Rows 1 to 4 form the pattern.

MOSS STITCH

Multiple of 2 sts plus 1

All rows: K1, * p1, k1, rep from * to end.

MOSS STITCH RIB

Multiple of 11 sts plus 5

Row 1: K5, *[k1, p1] 3 times, k5; rep from * to end.

Row 2: *P5, [p1, k1] 3 times; rep from * to last 5 sts, p5.

Rows 1 to 2 form the pattern.

MISTAKE RIB

Multiple of 4 sts plus 3.

All rows: *K2, p2; rep from * to last 3 sts, k2, p1.

RIPPLE STRIPE

Multiple of 8 sts plus 1

Row 1 (right side): K4, *p1, k7; rep from * to last 5 sts, p1, k4.

Row 2: P3, *k3, p5; rep from * to last 6 sts, k3, p3.

Row 3: K2, *p2, k1, p2, k3; rep from * to last 2 sts, k2.

Row 4: P1, *k2, p3, k2, p1; rep from * to end.

Row 5: K1, *p1, k5, p1, k1; rep from * to end.

Row 6: P.

Rows 1 to 6 form the pattern.

GARTER STITCH RIDGES

Any number of stitches

Row 1 (right side): K.

Row 2: P.

Rows 3 and 4: As rows 1 and 2.

Rows 5 to 10: P.

Rows 1 to 10 form the pattern.

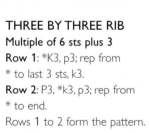

LADDER
Worked over 11 sts on a background of st st
Row 1 (right side): P2, k7, p2.
Row 2: K2, p7, k2.
Rows 3 and 4: As rows 1 and 2.
Row 5: P.
Row 6: As row 2.
Row 7: As row 1.
Rows 8 and 9: As rows 6 and 7.
Row 10: K.
Rows 1 to 10 form the pattern.

THREE BY THREE RIB
Multiple of 6 sts plus 3
Row 1: *K3, p3; rep from * to last 3 sts, k3.
Row 2: P3, *k3, p3; rep from * to end.
Rows 1 to 2 form the pattern.

SEEDED TEXTURE
Multiple of 5 sts plus 2
Row 1 (right side): K2, *p3, k2; rep from * to end.
Row 2: P.
Row 3: *P3, k2; rep from * to last 2 sts, p2.
Row 4: P.
Rows 1 to 4 form the pattern.

BASKETWEAVE
Multiple of 8 sts plus 3
Row 1 (right side): K.
Row 2: K4, p3, *k5, p3; rep from * to last 4 sts, k4.
Row 3: P4, k3, * p5, k3; rep from * to last 4 sts, p4.
Row 4: As row 2.
Row 5: K.
Row 6: P3, *k5, p3; rep from * to end.
Row 7: K3, *p5, k3; rep from * to end.
Row 8: As row 6.
Rows 1 to 8 form the pattern.

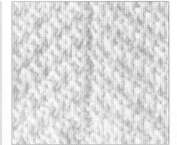

CHEVRON RIB
Multiple of 18 sts plus 1
Row 1 (right side): P1, *k1, p2, k2, p2, k1, p1; rep from * to end.
Row 2: *K3, p2, k2, p2, k1, [p2, k2] twice; rep from * to last st, k1.
Row 3: *[P2, k2] twice, p3, k2, p2, k2, p1; rep from * to last st, p1.
Row 4: *K1, p2, k2, p2, k5, p2, k2, p2; rep from * to last st, k1.
Rows 1 to 4 form the pattern.

SEED STITCH
Multiple of 4 sts
Row 1: *K3, p1; rep from * to end.
Row 2: P.
Row 3: K.
Row 4: P.
Row 5: K1, *p1, k3;* rep from * to last 3 sts, p1, k2.
Row 6: P.
Row 7: K.
Rows 1 to 7 form the pattern.

SQUARE LATTICE
Multiple of 14 sts plus 2
Row 1 (right side): K.
Rows 2, 4 and 6: P2, *[k1, p1] twice, k1, p2; rep from * to end.
Rows 3, 5, and 7: K3, *p1, k1, P1, k4; rep from * to last 3 sts, k3.
Row 8: P2, *k12, p2; rep from * to end.
Row 9: K2, *p12; rep from * to end.
Row 10: P.
Rows 11, 13, and 15: K2, *[p1, k1] twice, p1, k2; rep from * to end.
Rows 12, 14, and 16: P3, *k1, p1, k1, p4; rep from * to last 3 sts, p3.
Row 17: P7, *k2, p12; rep from * to last 9 sts, k2, p7.
Row 18: K7, *p2, k12; rep from * to last 9 sts, p2, k7.
Rows 1 to 18 form the pattern.

DIAMOND BROCADE
Multiple of 8 sts plus 1
Row 1 (right side): K4, *p1, k7; rep from * to last 5 sts, p1, k4.
Row 2: P3, *k1, p1, k1, p5; rep from * to last 6 sts, k1, p1, k1, p3.
Row 3: K2, *p1, k3; rep from * to last 3 sts, p1, k2.
Row 4: P1, *k1, p5, k1, p1; rep from * to end.
Row 5: *P1, k7; rep from * to last st, p1.
Row 6: As row 4.
Row 7: As row 3.
Row 8: As row 2.
Rows 1 to 8 form the pattern.

FRINGE BENEFITS

The simplest of patterns—k1, p1 rib—translates into a scarf that's a fashion statement with its wealth of fabulous fringe on one of its long sides. The soft alpaca-rich yarn is gentle against the skin when you have to wrap up warm on a windy, wintry day.

❖ SIZES
One size: 80" x 7½" (203 x 19 cm) excluding fringe

❖ MATERIALS
Yarn Bulky 60% wool/30% alpaca/10% acrylic (approx 109 yds/100 m per 100 g). 5 x 100 g balls
Needles One pair No. 11 (8 mm) or size to obtain gauge
Notions Crochet hook

❖ GAUGE
21 sts and 14 rows = 4" (10 cm) in rib pattern

❖ SKILLS USED
Rib st (p30), fringe tassels (p35)

See pages 18–19 for knitting terms.

SCARF

Use a slip-stitch selvage (see page 14) to give a firm edge.

Cast on 40 sts. Work in k1, p1 rib until work measures 80" (187.5 cm). Bind off in rib.

FINISHING

Make approximately 106 5-inch (13 cm) fringe tassels and space evenly every ¾" (2 cm) on one long side of scarf. Steam lightly.

Alternatively, if you wanted a more sedate scarf, say for a male friend, finish the shorter ends with fringe tassels.

A completely separate look will be achieved using plump tassels—in the same or a contrasting shade.

MAKING A FRINGE TASSEL

1 *Wrap yarn around a cardboard rectangle slightly deeper than desired length of fringe. Cut along one edge to make the strands. Take several strands and fold.*

2 *With a crochet hook, draw loop of strands through edge stitch, then pull cut ends through loop to form a loose knot; adjust. When all the tassels are in place, trim evenly.*

MAKING A PLUMP TASSEL

1 *Wrap yarn around cardboard cut to desired length. Thread length of yarn under top loops, and tie tightly; leave one end long. Cut through yarn at lower edge.*

2 *Hide knot and short end of yarn under tassel strands. Wind long end tightly around strands to form a neat top. Thread needle with long end of yarn and push under binding and out through top of tassel. Trim ends if necessary.*

TWISTED RIB HAT

All you need to knit up this warm winter hat is a single ball of yarn and a pair of needles. The pompoms, while easy to make, are optional. Using a twisted rib stitch, knitting into the back of the knit stitch and purling as usual, ensures that the hat is certain to hold its shape and fit the forehead better.

❖ **SIZES**
One size: To fit average head, 19" (48 cm) circumference

❖ **MATERIALS**
Yarn Super Bulky 100% merino wool (approx 187 yds/180 m per 100 g). 1 x 100 g ball.
Scraps of contrasting color for pompom (optional)
Needles One pair No. 17 (12 mm) or size to obtain gauge
Notions Tapestry needle

❖ **GAUGE**
8 sts and 11 rows to 4" (10 cm) over stockinette stitch

❖ **SKILLS USED**
Stockinette st (p12), twisted rib st (p30), decreasing (p22), seams (p27), pompoms (p37)

See pages 18–19 for knitting terms.

TWISTED RIB HAT
BRIM
Using main color, cast on 40 stitches.
Work 8 rows in twisted rib: k1b, p1.
Work 8 rows st st.

SHAPE CROWN
Row 1 (RS): (K7, K3 tog) 4 times—32 sts.
Row 2: Purl.
Row 3: (K5, K3 tog) 4 times—24 sts.
Row 4: Purl.
Row 5: (K3, K3 tog) 4 times—16 sts.
Row 6: Purl.
Row 7: (K1, K3 tog) 4 times—8 sts.
Row 8: Purl.
Break yarn (leaving enough to sew up hat)
and thread through remaining sts. Pull up
tightly and secure.

FINISHING
Stitch back seam on inside. Press lightly.
Make pompom and attach to top of hat.

MAKING POMPOMS

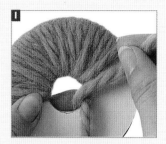

1 Cut two cardboard circles to desired size of finished pompom. In the center of each circle, cut a hole about one third of the total diameter. Place the circles together. Wrap the yarn as shown.

2 Continue wrapping yarn until the central holes are completely filled. If you run out of yarn, take a new length, continue wrapping, and leave the ends dangling at the outer edge.

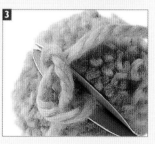

3 Cut through the yarn around the outer edge. Ease the circles slightly apart and wrap a length of yarn tightly around the central strands a few times. Secure with a firm knot. Pull off cardboard circles. Fluff out pompom, and trim with sharp scissors. Use dangling threads to attach to garment.

Trimmed and finished pompom

CAMISOLE

Not all knitting is about big woolen sweaters! This fun top knits up quickly, as the bodice is worked in one piece. It's fastened at the back by a length of twisted cord laced through the edges.

❖ **SIZES**
XS, S, M, L, XL: To fit bust 32 (34, 36, 38, 40)" (81 [86, 91.5, 96.5, 101.5] cm). Finished size: Bust 28 (30, 32, 34, 36)" (71 [76, 81, 86, 91.5] cm)

❖ **MATERIALS**
Yarn *Brocade tape 50%cotton/40%rayon/10% nylon (approx. 130 yds/144 m per 100 g). 2 (2, 2, 3, 3) x 100 g hanks*
Needles *One pair each No. 6 (4 mm) and No. 10 (6 mm) or size to obtain gauge*
Notions *Tapestry needle, crochet hook*

❖ **GAUGE**
13 sts and 18 rows = 4" (10 cm) over moss stitch

❖ **SKILLS USED**
Moss st (p31), twisted cord (p69), openwork (p86)

See pages 18–19 for knitting terms.

CAMISOLE
BACK AND FRONT
(One piece)

With No. 6 needles cast on 358 (382, 410, 434, 462) sts.

FRILLY EDGE

Row 1(RS): K1 *k2, slip 1st st over 2nd st on RH needle, rep from * to last st, k1.
Row 2: Purl.
Row 3: Work as row 1.
Row 4: Purl—91 (97, 104, 110, 117)sts. Change to No. 10 needles and work in moss st (see page 31) until piece measures 10 (10, 10, 11, 11)" (25.5 [25.5, 25.5, 28, 28] cm) from cast on edge. Bind off.

FINISHING
SHOULDER STRAPS

Make 2 15" (38 cm) (or size to fit) twisted cords (see page 69). Attach one cord to top edge, one end 4 (4, 4, 4½ 4½)" (11.5 [11.5, 11.5, 13, 13] cm) from center back and other end 10 (11, 12, 12.5, 13)" (25 [28, 30.5, 32, 33] cm) from center back. Repeat with other cord.

BACK FASTENINGS

Make 2 24" (61 cm) twisted cords. Sew cords to back above frilly edge. Using crochet hook, lace the 2 straps evenly at approx 1¾" (4.5 cm) intervals up center back and tie in a bow at top. Steam lightly.

28 (30, 32, 34, 36)"

10 (10, 10, 11, 11)"

CABLE KNITTING

Cables can transform an otherwise simple knitted garment into something really special. They can be used as single panels or be repeated to form an all-over pattern.

Heavily textured patterns can add to a sweater's warmth and durability. Learning to make cables is within the abilities of every knitter. If you are adding cable panels to a plain sweater pattern, you must remember that cables tend to decrease the overall width, so plan the pattern and yarn requirements accordingly.

CABLING BASICS

The basis of all cable patterns is a simple technique whereby stitches are crossed over another group of stitches in the same row. Some of the stitches making up the cable are held at the back (or front) of the work on a special cable needle, while the other stitches are knitted. Then the stitches on the cable needle are knitted, thereby creating a twist.

MAKING CABLES

The cables shown on page 41 are six stitches wide; these six stitches are knitted on the right side and purled on the wrong side. The stitches on either side of the cable are purled on the right side and knitted on the wrong side, i.e. in reverse stockinette stitch. The length between the twists can be changed as desired; commonly they are crossed every sixth or eighth row. The cables shown here are crossed at the eighth row, having started with a wrong-side row.

Two lines of large double cables make a bold vertical pattern on this knitted backpack (see pages 48–49).

RIGHT-HAND CABLE

Holding the stitches on a cable needle at the front of the work always produces a right-over-left cable.

1 *Slip the first three stitches onto a cable needle and hold at the front of the work.*

2 *Then knit the next three stitches on the main needle.*

3 *Finally, knit the three stitches held on the cable needle.*

SPECIAL EQUIPMENT

Cable needles are short double-pointed needles that allow you to hold the stitches to be twisted at the front or back of the work. They can be straight or curved. The curved needle holds the stitches more firmly and keeps them from slipping off.

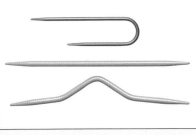

LEFT-HAND CABLE

Holding the stitches on a cable needle at the back of the work always produces a left-over-right cable.

1 *Slip the first three stitches onto a cable needle and hold at the back of the work.*

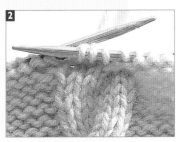

2 *Then knit the next three stitches on the main needle.*

3 *Finally, knit the three stitches held on the cable needle.*

CABLE TERMS

The instructions in a knitting pattern for the left-hand cable shown here would read C6B (cable 6 back). For the right-hand, they would read C6F (cable 6 front). The instruction C4B would mean you slipped two stitches onto the cable needle, which would be held at the back while you knitted the next two stitches before knitting those on the cable needle. Similarly, the instruction C8F would mean you slipped four stitches onto the cable needle, held at the front while you knitted four stitches, then the stitches from the cable needle.

CROSS RIB CABLE

Multiple of 11 sts

Row 1 (wrong side): K2, [p1, k1] 4 times, k1.

Row 2: P2, [k1 tbl, p1] 4 times, p1.

Rows 3 to 6: Rep rows 1 and 2 twice.

Row 7: As row 1.

Row 8: P2, slip next 4 sts to front on cable needle, [k1tbl, p1] twice from main needle, [k1tbl, p1] twice from cable needle, p1.

Rows 9 to 12: Rep rows 1 and 2 twice.

Rows 1 to 12 form the pattern.

LARGE DOUBLE CABLE

Worked over 20 sts on a background of reverse st st

Row 1 (right side): K.

Row 2: P.

Row 3: C10B, C10F.

Row 4: P.

Rows 5 to 12: Rep rows 1 and 2 four times.

Rows 1 to 12 form the pattern.

CLAW PATTERN

Worked over 9 sts on a background of reverse st st

Special abbreviations

Cross 4L (Cross 4 Left): Slip next st onto cn and hold at front of work, knit next 3 sts from left needle then knit st from cn.

Cross 4R (Cross 4 Right): Slip next 3 sts onto cn and hold at back of work, knit next st from left needle then knit sts from cn.

Downward claw

Row 1 (right side): K.

Row 2: P.

Row 3: Cross 4L, k1, Cross 4R.

Row 4: P.

Rows 1 to 4 form the pattern.

Upward claw

Row 1 (right side): K.

Row 2: P.

Row 3: Cross 4R, k1, Cross 4L.

Row 4: P.

Rows 1 to 4 form the pattern.

TELESCOPE LATTICE

Worked over 12 sts on a background of st st

Row 1 and every alt row (wrong side): P.

Row 2: K.

Row 4: *C4B, k4, C4F; rep from * to end.

Row 6: K.

Row 8: *K2, C4F, C4B, k2; rep from * to end.

Rows 1 to 8 form the pattern.

NINE STITCH PLAIT

Worked over 9 sts on a background of reverse st st

Downward plait

Row 1 (right side): K.

Row 2 and every alt row: P.

Row 3: C6F, k3.

Row 5: K.

Row 7: K3, C6B.

Row 8: P.

Upward plait

Row 1 (right side): K.

Row 2 and every alt row: P.

Row 3: C6B, k3.

Row 5: K.

Row 7: K3, C6F.

Row 8: P.

Rows 1 to 8 form each pattern.

DOUBLE CROSSOVER

Worked over 16 sts on a background of reverse st st

Special abbreviations

T3B (Twist 3 Back): Slip next st onto cn and hold at back, k next 2 sts from left needle, then p st from cn.

T3F (Twist 3 Front): Slip next 2 sts onto cn and hold at front of work, purl next st from left needle, then knit sts from cn.

Row 1 (right side): K2, p4, k4, p4, k2.

Row 2: P2, k4, p4, k4, p2.

Row 3: K2, p4, C4B, p4, k2.

Row 4: As row 2.

Row 5: [T3F, p2, T3B] twice.

Row 6: K1, p2, [k2, p2] 3 times, k1.

Row 7: P1, T3F, T3B, p2, T3F, T3B, p1.

Row 8: K2, p4, k4, p4, k2.

Row 9: P2, C4B, p4, C4B, p2.

Row 10: As row 8.

Row 11: P2, k4, p4, k4, p2.

Rows 12 and 13: As rows 8 and 9.

Row 14: As row 8.

Row 15: P1, T3B, T3F, p2, T3B, T3F, p1.

Row 16: As row 6.

Row 17: [T3B, p2, T3F] twice.

Rows 18 and 19: As rows 2 and 3.

Row 20: As row 2.

Rows 1 to 20 form the pattern.

MEDALLION MOSS CABLE

Worked over 13 sts on a background of reverse st st

Row 1 (right side): K4, [p1, k1] 3 times, k3.

Row 2: P3, [k1, p1] 4 times, p2.

Rows 3 and 4: As rows 1 and 2.

Row 5: C6F, k1, C6B.

Row 6: P.

Row 7: K.

Rows 8 to 11: Rep rows 6 and 7 twice.

Row 12: P.

Row 13: C6B, k1, C6F.

Row 14: As row 2.

Row 15: As row 1.

Row 16: As row 2.

Rows 1 to 16 form the pattern.

SMALL TWIST STITCH CABLE

Multiple of 8 sts plus 3

Row 1 (right side): *K3, p1, k1tbl, p1, k1tbl, p1; rep from * to last 3 sts, k3.

Row 2: P3, *k1, p1tbl, k1, p1tbl, k1, p3; rep from * to end.

Rows 3 to 6: Rep rows 1 and 2 twice.

Row 7: *K3, p1, slip next 2 sts to front on cn, k1tbl, p1, k1tbl from cn, p1; rep from * to last 3 sts, k3.

Row 8: As row 2.

Rows 1 to 8 form the pattern.

OPENWORK AND TWIST

Multiple of 15 sts plus 12

Special abbreviation

T4LR (Twist 4 Left and Right): Slip next 3 sts onto cn and hold at back of work, knit next st from left needle then slip the first st on cn back to left needle, p2 from cn then k1 from left needle.

Row 1 (right side): P1, T4LR, p2, T4LR, p1, *k1, yo, sl 1, k1, psso, p1, T4LR, p2, T4LR, p1; rep from * to end.

Row 2: K1, p1, [k2, p1] 3 times, k1, *p3, k1, p1, [k2, p1] 3 times, k1; rep from * to end.

Row 3: P1, k1, p2, T4LR, p2, k1, p1, *k2tog, yo, k1, p1, k1, p2, T4LR, p2, k1, p1; rep from * to end.

Row 4: As row 2.

Rows 1 to 4 form the pattern.

LITTLE WAVE

Multiple of 7 sts plus 4

Row 1 (right side): K.

Row 2: P4, *k2, p5; rep from * to end.

Row 3: K4, *C2F, k5; rep from * to end.

Row 4: P4, *k1, p1, k1, p4; rep from * to end.

Row 5: *K5, C2F; rep from * to last 4 sts, k4.

Row 6: *P5, k2; rep from * to last 4 sts, p4.

Row 7: K.

Row 8: As row 6.

Row 9: *K5, C2B; rep from * to last 4 sts, k4.

Row 10: As row 4.

Row 11: K4, *C2B, k5; rep from * to end.

Row 12: As row 2.

Rows 1 to 12 form the pattern.

HONEYCOMB

Multiple of 8 sts

Row 1 (right side): *C4B, C4F; rep from * to end of panel.

Row 2: P.

Row 3: K.

Row 4: P.

Row 5: *C4F, C4B; rep from * to end of panel.

Row 6: P.

Row 7: K.

Row 8: P.

Rows 1 to 8 form the pattern.

BRAID CABLE

Multiple of 8 (min. 16 sts) worked on a background of reverse st st. Shown worked over 24 sts

Row 1 (right side): K.

Row 2 and every alt row: P.

Row 3: K.

Row 5: *C8B; rep from * to end of panel.

Row 7: K.

Row 9: K.

Row 11: *C8F; rep from * to end of panel.

Row 12: P.

Rows 1 to 12 form the pattern.

STRIPED MEDALLION CABLE

Worked over 16 sts on a background of reverse st st

Special abbreviations

T8B rib (Twist 8 Back rib): Slip next 4 sts onto cn and hold at back of work, k1, p2, k1 from left-hand needle, then k1, p2, k1 from cn.

T8F rib (Twist 8 Front rib): Slip next 4 sts onto cn and hold at front of work, k1, p2, k1 from left-hand needle, then k1, p2, k1 from cn.

Row 1 (right side): K1, p2, [k2, p2] 3 times, k1.

Row 2: P1, k2, [p2, k2] 3 times, p1.

Row 3: T8B rib, T8F rib.

Row 4: As row 2.

Rows 5 to 14: Rep rows 1 and 2 five times.

Row 15: T8F rib, T8B rib.

Row 16: As row 2.

Rows 17 to 24: Rep rows 1 and 2 four times.

Rows 1 to 24 form the pattern.

INTERLACED CABLES

Multiple of 8 sts plus 10

Special abbreviations

T4B (Twist 4 Back): Slip next 2 sts onto cn and hold at back of work, knit next 2 sts from left needle, then purl sts from cn.

T4F (Twist 4 Front): Slip next 2 sts onto cn and hold at front of work, purl next 2 sts from left needle, then knit sts from cn.

Row 1 (right side): P3, k4, *p4, k4; rep from * to last 3 sts, p3.

Row 2: K3, p4, *k4, p4; rep from * to last 3 sts, k3.

Row 3: P3, C4B, *p4, C4B; rep from * to last 3 sts, p3.

Row 4: As row 2.

Rows 5 to 8: As rows 1 to 4.

Row 9: P1, *T4B, T4F; rep from * to last st, p1.

Row 10: K1, p2, k4, *p4, k4; rep from * to last 3 sts, p2, k1.

Row 11: P1, k2, p4, *C4F, p4; rep from * to last 3 sts, k2, p1.

Row 12: As row 10.

Row 13: P1, *T4F, T4B; rep from * to last st, p1.

Rows 14 and 15: As rows 2 and 3.

Row 16: As row 2.

Rows 1 to 16 form the pattern.

CHAIN CABLE

Worked over 8 sts on a background of reverse st st

Row 1 (right side): K.

Row 2: P.

Row 3: C4B, C4F.

Row 4: P.

Rows 5 and 6: As rows 1 and 2.

Row 7: C4F, C4B.

Row 8: P.

Rows 1 to 8 form the pattern.

ALTERNATING BRAID CABLE

Worked over 6 sts on a background of reverse st st

Row 1 (wrong side): P.

Row 2: K.

Row 3: P.

Row 4: C4B, k2.

Row 5: P.

Row 6: K2, C4F.

Rows 3 to 6 form the pattern.

SNAKE CABLE

Worked over 8 sts on a background of reverse st st

Row 1 (right side): K8.

Row 2: P8.

Row 3: C8B.

Row 4: P8.

Rows 5 to 10: Rep rows 1 and 2 three times.

Row 11: C8F.

Row 12: P8.

Rows 13 to 16: Rep rows 1 and 2 twice.

Rows 1 to 16 form the pattern.

FLAPS OR NO FLAPS?

Your choice of two warm winter hats. Both fit the head closely but the pointed version has extra-warm earflaps. Use bright, bold colors that will stand out on the ski slope and bring some cheer to a gray day.

❖ **SIZE**
One size: To fit average head, 20" (51 cm) circumference

❖ **MATERIALS**
Yarn Knitting worsted 100% merino wool (131 yds/ 120 m per 50 g)
Yarn is used double throughout
Hat with flaps: 3 x 50 g balls
No flaps: 2 x 50 g balls
Needles One pair No. 8 (5 mm) and one pair No. 10½ (6.5 mm) or sizes to obtain gauge, cable needle
Notions Tapestry needle, crochet hook

❖ **GAUGE**
18 sts and 19 rows = 4" (10 cm) over cable pattern

❖ **SKILLS USED**
Garter st (p10), decreasing (p22), seams (p27), fringe tassels (p35), cable knitting (p40), yarn over increases (p87)

See pages 18–19 for knitting terms.

CABLE PATTERN

C4F: Slip 2 sts purlwise one at a time to cable needle (cn) and hold at front of work, k2, k2 from cn.

Row 1: *P2, k4; rep from * to last 2 sts, p2.
Row 2: *K2, p4; rep from * to last 2 sts, k2.
Row 3: *P2, C4F; rep from * to last 2 sts, p2.
Row 4: *K2, p4; rep from * to last 2 sts, k2.
Repeat rows 1 to 4.

HAT WITH FLAPS
BRIM

Using No. 8 needles, cast on 86 sts. Work 6 rows in garter st.

Change to No. 10½ needles and work in cable pattern until work measures 7" (17.5 cm) from cast-on edge ending on patt row 2.

SHAPE CROWN

Row 1: *P2tog; C4F; repeat from * to last 2 sts, p2tog—71 sts.
Row 2: *K1, p1, p2tog, p1; repeat from * to last st, k1—57 sts.
Row 3: *K2tog; rep from * to last st, k1—29 sts.
Row 4: Purl.
Row 5: *K2tog; rep from * to last st, k1—15 sts.
Row 6: Purl.
Row 7: *K2tog; rep from * to last st, k1—8 sts.
Rows 8–11: Work in st st.

Row 12: P2tog across row. Break off yarn, thread through remaining sts and secure firmly on inside.

EAR FLAPS

Make 2.
Using No. 8 needles, cast on 2 sts.
Row 1 (RS): K2.
Row 2: Yarn over needle to make a st (yo), k2.
Row 3: Yo, k3.
Row 4: Yo, k4.
Row 5: Yo, k5.
Cont as above, making one yo at beg of every row until there are 20 sts. Work even in garter st until flap measures 7" (17.5 cm) from point. Bind off. Make second flap.

FINISHING

With tapestry needle and yarn, stitch back seam on inside. Stitch ear flaps onto hat 3" (7.5 cm) from back seam. Make 6 8½" (21.5 cm) fringe tassels (see page 35) and attach three tassels to point of each ear flap. Steam lightly.

NO FLAPS
BRIM

Work as Hat with Flaps up to row 7 of crown.
Row 8: Purl.
Break off yarn; thread through remaining sts and secure firmly.

FINISHING

Make 4 8½" (21.5 cm) fringe tassels (see page 35) and attach to crown. Steam lightly.

COTTON CABLE BACKPACK

This hands-free carryall knits up fast and the cotton denim yarn makes it hard-wearing as well. A bold cable pattern adds interest to the front side of the bag, which is just two rectangles joined together with a cord threaded through the top.

❖ **SIZES**
One size: 11" wide and 13" long (28 x 33 cm)

❖ **MATERIALS**
Yarn Medium weight 100% cotton denim (101 yds/ 93 m per 50 g). 4 x 50 g balls
Needles One pair each No. 4 (3.25 mm) and No. 6 (4 mm) or size to obtain gauge, cable needle
Notions Tapestry needle

❖ **GAUGE**
20 sts and 32 rows = 4" (10 cm) over stockinette stitch using No. 6 needles

❖ **SKILLS USED**
Garter st (p10), stockinette st (p12), decreasing (p22), blocking and pressing (p26), seams (p27), cable knitting (p40), twisted cord (p69), eyelets (p89)

See pages 18–19 for knitting terms.

COTTON CABLE BACKPACK
DOUBLE CABLE STITCH

C10B: Place 5 sts on cable needle (cn) and hold at back of work, k5, k5 from cn
C10F: Place 5 sts on cn and hold at front of work, k5, k5 from cn.

BACK

With No. 6 needles cast on 56 sts.
Work in st st until piece measures 12" (30.5 cm).
Change to No. 4 needles and work **4 rows garter st, then 2 rows st st.
Next row (eyelet row): K3 *yo, k2tog, k5; repeat from * to last 4 st, k4.
Next row: Purl.
Work 4 rows garter st.
Bind off.

FRONT

With No. 6 needles cast on 78 sts. Work 2 rows in st st.
Row 1 (RS): P13, k20, p12, k20, p13.
Row 2: K13, p20, k12, p20, k13.
Row 3: P13, C10B, C10F, p12, C10B, C10F, p13.
Row 4: K13, p20, k12, p20, k13.
Rows 5, 7, 9, 11: P13, k20, p12, k20, p13.
Rows 6, 8, 10, 12: K13, p20, k12, p20, k13.
Repeat rows 1–12 until piece measures 12" (30.5 cm), ending on RS row.
Next row (WS) and continuing in pattern: *work 1, work 2 tog, work 2, work 2 tog; rep from * 11 times, work 1–56 sts.
Change to No. 4 needles and work as for Back from ** to end.

FINISHING

Block and press on WS. Using backstitch on edge of work, join 3 seams, leaving top edge open. Make 65" (165 cm) twisted cord (see page 69). Thread cord through the eyelets; start at the side seam, once around, then back again to finish on other side seam. Knot the ends of the cord and cut to form tassels. Secure the tassels at the bottom corners of the bag.

RAISED PATTERNS

A variety of dramatic effects can be achieved by using stitches to create patterns that stand out from the background. These stitches are produced by increasing and decreasing techniques, and can sometimes be combined with twist or cable stitches.

Raised stitches come in all sizes, and can be worked in rows or panels, or as all-over textures. They can also be combined with lace patterns and cables. Bobbles, popcorns, buds, and clusters are some of the most popular patterns.

A garment that has many motifs will be much thicker and heavier than a plainly knitted one, and will use more yarn. For this reason, traditional outdoor wear, such as a fisherman's sweater, is often heavily patterned. To make these stitches, you need only to master the technique of multiple increases in a single stitch.

Trinity stitch creates a surface texture of delicate, soft bumps, just right for this appealing pink sweater (right) with its ribbon-tied front (see page 54).

BOBBLES

A large cluster of stitches that is independent of the knitted ground, a bobble can be worked in stockinette or reverse stockinette stitch. It is formed by increasing into a single stitch so that three (four, or five) additional stitches for a small (medium, or large) bobble are made. Work backward and forward on these stitches only. Finally, decrease these extra stitches to the original one. The increases can be made in two ways—using the yarn-over method or working into the front and back of a stitch. The stitches on either side must be worked firmly. Bobbles will make the edge uneven, so start a few stitches in to make the sewing up easier.

YARN-OVER INCREASES

Knit up to your chosen stitch then make a yarn over—insert your right-hand needle into the stitch and knit as usual but do not discard. To make 5 new stitches (a total of 6 stitches), yarn over and knit into the same stitch 3 more times; slip last stitch onto right needle. This may be abbreviated as *yo, k1; rep from * twice (3, 4 times, etc.).

WORKING INTO FRONT AND BACK OF STITCH

Knit up to your chosen stitch then insert your right-hand needle into it. Leave the stitch on the needle as you knit first into the front and then the back the appropriate number of times. To increase 4 times, making 4 new stitches (a total of 5 stitches), knit into the front and back of the stitch twice and then knit into the front again. Occasionally, an instruction will ask you to increase by alternately knitting and purling into the stitch.

Small bobble

Medium bobble

Large bobble

MAKING BOBBLES

1 For a medium bobble, work up to the chosen stitch. Then increase 3 times into the stitch (4 sts altogether). (We've used the yarn-over method.)

2 Turn work and knit 4 stitches; turn work and purl 4 stitches; turn work and knit 4 stitches; turn work (3 rows of reverse stockinette stitch made).

3 Decrease by 3 stitches: Sl 2, k2tog, p2sso; bobble made. Continue in pattern.

4 The completed bobble on a stockinette stitch ground.

MOCK CABLE

Multiple of 5 sts plus 2

Row 1 (right side): P2, *sl 1, k2, psso, p2; rep from * to end.

Row 2: K2, *p1, yo, p1, k2; rep from * to end.

Row 3: P2, *k3, p2; rep from * to end.

Row 4: K2, *p3, k2; rep from * to end.

Rows 1 to 4 form the pattern.

HAZEL NUT

Multiple of 4 sts plus 3

HN: K1 without slipping st off left needle, yo, then k1 once more into same st.

Note: Sts should only be counted after rows 4, 5, 6, 10, 11, or 12.

Row 1 (right side): P3, *HN, p3; rep from * to end.

Row 2: K3, *p3, k3; rep from * to end.

Row 3: P3, *k3, p3; rep from * to end.

Row 4: K3, *p3tog, k3; rep from * to end.

Rows 5 and 11: P.

Rows 6 and 12: K.

Row 7: P1, *HN, p3; rep from * to last 2 sts, HN, p1.

Row 8: K1, *p3, k3; rep from * to last 4 sts, p3, k1.

Row 9: P1, *k3, p3; rep from * to last 4 sts, k3, p1.

Row 10: K1, *p3tog, k3; rep from * to last 4 sts, p3tog, k1.

Rows 1 to 12 form the pattern.

SCATTERED BOBBLES

Multiple of 10 sts plus 5 worked on a background of st st

MB (Make Bobble): Knit into front, back and front of next st, turn and p3, turn and k3, turn and p3, turn and sl 1, k2tog, psso.

Rows 1 and 3: K.

Rows 2 and 4: P.

Row 5: K7, *MB, k9; rep from * to last 8 sts, MB, k7.

Rows 6, 8 and 10: P.

Rows 7 and 9: K.

Row 11: K2, *MB, k9; rep from * to last 3 sts, MB, k2.

Row 12: P.

Rows 1 to 12 form the pattern.

HONEYCOMB STITCH

Multiple of 4 sts

C2B or C2F (Cross 2 Back or Front): K into back (or front) of 2nd st on needle, then k first st, slipping both sts off needle at same time.

Row 1 (right side): *C2F, C2B; rep from * to end.

Row 2: P.

Row 3: *C2B, C2F; rep from * to end.

Row 4: P.

Rows 1 to 4 form the pattern.

VERTICAL BOBBLE AND STRIPE

Multiple of 10 sts plus 5

MB (Make Bobble): Work [k1, p1, k1, p1, k1] into the next st, turn and k5, turn and k5tog.

Row 1 (right side): P2, k1, *p4, k1; rep from * to last 2 sts, p2.

Row 2: K2, p1, *k4, p1; rep from * to last 2 sts, k2.

Row 3: P2, *MB, p4, k1, p4; rep from * to last 3 sts, MB, p2.

Row 4: As row 2.

Rows 5 to 20: rep rows 1 to 4 four times.

Row 21: As row 1.

Row 22: As row 2.

Row 23: P2, *k1, p4, MB, p4; rep from * to last 3 sts, k1, p2.

Row 24: As row 2.

Rows 25 to 40: Rep rows 21 to 24 four times.

Rows 1 to 40 form the pattern.

GARTER STITCH CHEVRON

Multiple of 11 sts

Rows 1 to 5: Knit.

Row 6 (right side): *K2tog, k2, knit into front and back of each of the next 2 sts, k3, ssk; rep from * to end.

Row 7: P.

Rows 8 to 11: Rep rows 6 and 7 twice.

Row 12: Same as row 6.

Rows 1 to 12 form the pattern.

BUD STITCH

Multiple of 6 sts plus 5

Note: Sts should only be counted after row 6 or 12.

Row 1 (right side): P5, *k1, yo, p5; rep from * to end.

Row 2: K5, *p2, k5; rep from * to end.

Row 3: P5, *k2, p5; rep from * to end.

Rows 4 and 5: As rows 2 and 3.

Row 6: K5, *p2tog, k5; rep from * to end.

Row 7: P2, *k1, yo, p5; rep from * to last 3 sts, k1, yo, p2.

Row 8: K2, *p2, k5; rep from * to last 4 sts, p2, k2.

Row 9: P2, *k2, p5; rep from * to last 4 sts, k2, p2.

Rows 10 and 11: As rows 8 and 9.

Row 12: K2, *p2tog, k5; rep from * to last 4 sts, p2tog, k2.

Rows 1 to 12 form the pattern.

BOBBLE AND RIDGE

Multiple of 6 sts plus 5

MB (Make Bobble): Knit into front, back and front of next st, turn and p3, turn and k3, turn and p3, turn and sl 1, k2tog, psso.

Row 1 (right side): K.

Rows 2: P.

Row 3: K5, *MB, k5; rep from * to end.

Row 4: P.

Row 5: K2, *MB, k5; rep from * to last 2 sts, k2.

Rows 6, 7, and 8: As rows 2, 3, and 4.

Row 9: P.

Row 10: K.

Rows 1 to 10 form the pattern.

TRINITY STITCH

Multiple of 4 sts plus 2

M2 (Make 2 sts): K1, p1, k1 all into next st.

Row 1 (right side): P.

Row 2: K1, *M2, p3tog; rep from * to last st, k1.

Row 3: P.

Row 4: K1, *p3tog, M2; rep from * to last st, k1.

Rows 1 to 4 form the pattern.

BUBBLE STITCH

Note: Slip all sts p-wise. Use reverse side of pattern as the right side (see above).

Row 1 (right side): K.

Row 2: P.

Row 3: P1, yb, sl 2, yf, *p6, yb, sl2, yf; rep from * to last st, p1.

Row 4: K1, yf, sl2, yb, *k6, yt, sl 2, yb; rep from * to last st, k1.

Rows 5 to 8: Rep rows 3 and 4 twice.

Row 9: K.

Row 10: P.

Row 11: P5, yb, sl 2, yf, *p6, yb, sl 2, yf; rep from * to last 5 sts, p5.

Row 12: K5, yf, sl 2, yb, *k6, yf, sl 2 yb; rep from * to last 5 sts, k5.

Rows 13 to 16: Rep rows 11 and 12 twice.

Rows 1 to 16 form the pattern.

FLIRTY SWEATER

This ribbon-fastening sweater is ideal for dressing up a simple evening outfit or as a lightweight top on warmer evenings. It is knitted in trinity stitch, a raised pattern, which gives it an interesting texture.

❖ SIZES

XS, S, M, L, XL: To fit bust 32 (34, 36, 38, 40)" (81 [86, 91.5, 96.5, 101.5] cm). Finished size: 32 (34, 36, 38, 40)" (81 [86, 91.5, 96.5, 101.5] cm)

❖ MATERIALS

Yarn Lightweight 100% mercerized cotton (approx 114 yds/105 m per 50 g). 13 (13, 14, 15, 16) x 50 g balls
Needles One pair No. 6 (4 mm) and one pair No. 3 (3 mm) or sizes to obtain gauge
Notions Tapestry needle, 80" (2 m) of 1" (2.5 cm) wide ribbon

❖ GAUGE

28 sts and 32 rows = 4" (10 cm) over trinity stitch

❖ SKILLS USED

Garter st (p10), increasing (p20), decreasing (p22), seams (p27), trinity st (p53), picking up sts (p88)

See pages 18–19 for knitting terms.

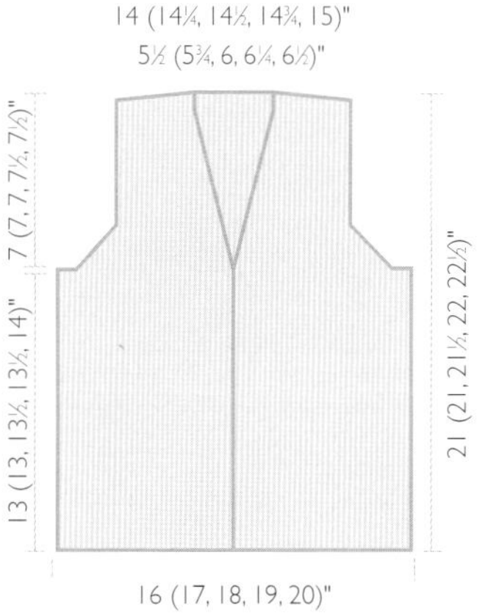
14 (14¼, 14½, 14¾, 15)"
5½ (5¾, 6, 6¼, 6½)"
7 (7, 7, 7½, 7½)"
13 (13, 13½, 13½, 14)"
21 (21, 21½, 22, 22½)"
16 (17, 18, 19, 20)"

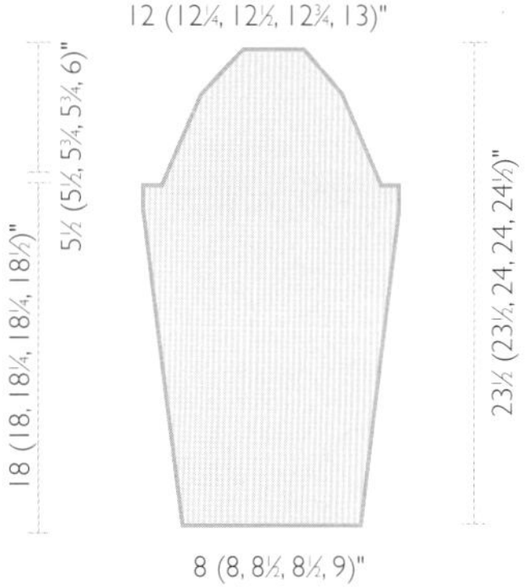
12 (12¼, 12½, 12¾, 13)"
5½ (5½, 5¾, 5¾, 6)"
18 (18, 18¼, 18¼, 18½)"
23½ (23½, 24, 24, 24½)"
8 (8, 8½, 8½, 9)"

FLIRTY SWEATER

BACK

Using No. 6 needles, cast on 114 (118, 126, 134, 142) sts. and work in trinity st (see page 53) until piece measures 13 (13, 13½, 13½, 14)" (33 [33, 34, 34, 35.5] cm) from cast-on edge ending on WS row.

ARMHOLE SHAPING

Keeping patt correct as set, bind off 3 (3, 4, 4, 5) sts at beg of next 2 rows and then dec 1 st at both ends of the next and foll alt rows 5 (6, 8, 11, 13) times—98 (100, 102, 104, 106) sts. Continue even in patt as set until the armhole measures 7 (7, 7, 7½, 7½)" (18 [18, 18, 19, 19] cm) ending on WS row.

SHOULDER SHAPING

Keeping patt correct as set, bind off 8 sts at the beginning of the next 4 rows and 7 sts at the beginning of the following 4 rows. Bind off remaining 38 (40, 42, 44, 46) sts.

LEFT FRONT

Using No. 6 needles, cast on 57 (59, 63, 67, 71) sts and work in trinity st until piece measures 13 (13, 13½, 13½, 14)" (33[33, 34, 34, 35.5] cm) from cast-on edge ending on WS row.

ARMHOLE AND NECK SHAPING

*Keeping patt correct as set, bind off 3 (3, 4, 4, 5) sts at beg of next row. Work 1 row. Then dec 1 st at beg of next and foll alt rows 5 (6, 8, 11, 13) times.

*At the same time dec 1 st at center front edge on first and then every alt row 10 (13, 16, 15, 18) times, then every 3rd row 8 (6, 4, 6, 4) times—30 sts.

Cont as set until work measures 20 (20, 20½, 21, 21½)" (51[51, 52, 53, 54.5] cm) ending on WS row.

SHOULDER SHAPING

Bind off 8 sts. Work 1 row. Bind off 8 sts. Work 1 row. Bind off 7 sts. Work 1 row. Bind off rem 7 sts.

RIGHT FRONT

Work as for Left Front, reversing all shapings.

SLEEVES

Using No. 3 needles, cast on 54 (54, 58, 58, 62) sts. Work 6 rows in garter stitch. Change to No. 6 needles and work in trinity st, inc 1 st at both ends of next and every 8th row 0 (7, 0, 5, 0) times, then every 9th row 12 (8, 12, 10, 8) times, then every 10th row 2 (0, 2, 0, 6) times—84 (86, 88, 90, 92) sts. Work even in patt as set until sleeve measures 18 (18, 18¼, 18¼, 18½)" (46[46, 46.5, 46.5, 47] cm) from cast-on edge, ending on WS row.

SLEEVE CAP SHAPING

Bind off 3 (3, 4, 4, 5) sts at beg of next 2 rows. Then dec 1 st at both ends of every alt row 16 (15, 17, 17, 19) times, then every row 10 (12, 10, 10, 8) times. Bind off remaining 26 (26, 26, 28, 28) sts.

LEFT FRONT BAND

Join shoulder seams. With right side of work facing, using No. 3 needles, starting at center back neck, pick up and knit 1 st for each stitch or row to bound-off edge of cardigan. Work 5 rows in garter stitch. Bind off.

RIGHT FRONT BAND

Work as for Left Front Band starting at cast-on edge up to center back neck.

FINISHING

Sew sleeve cap into armhole. Join side and sleeve seams in one line. Join front bands at center back. Steam lightly. Cut ribbon in half and sew one piece onto each front at start of neck shaping.

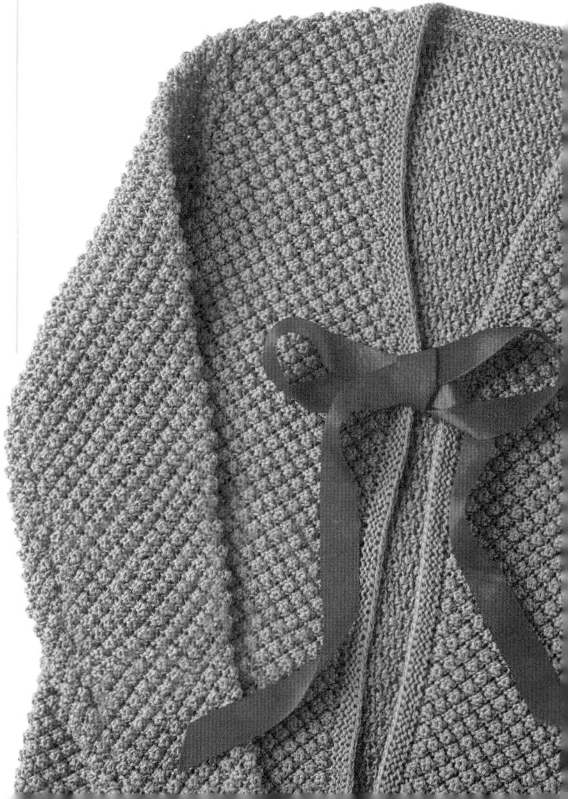

EMBROIDERY

Simple embroidery stitches add color and texture to a knitted garment. Some of the most popular stitches are shown here—from Swiss darning to squared filling stitch.

EMBROIDERY BASICS

It is often easier to embroider on knitting before the garment has been assembled, but after it has been blocked (see page 26). The key is to work with the knitted fabric and not against it. Do not pull the embroidery stitches too tight or the knitting will pucker, and always work with a blunt-ended tapestry needle or yarn needle to avoid splitting the knitted stitches. Embroider with a yarn of the same type and thickness as the knitting—if the embroidery yarn is too thin it will sink into the knitted stitches, and if it is too thick it will stretch the knitting and look lumpy. You can also use embroidery floss or tapestry wool instead of knitting yarn. These products are sold in small, economical amounts and come in a wide range of beautiful colors. Bear in mind that you may need to work with several strands to match the thickness of the knitting yarn.

Swiss darning follows the same stitch pattern as the knitting, and can be used instead of color knitting (see pages 60–65) to work motifs, or in combination with color knitting to add areas of color. Cross stitch is quick and easy and a great way to create patterns. Chain and stem stitch are both simple to do and can be used to make a raised line on the surface of your knitting. Couching is a good way to get a raised line on your work, by laying a thicker thread or yarn onto your knitting.

Bullion knots provide interesting texture. Squared filling stitch can be used to cover large areas and to fill in shapes outlined by other embroidery stitches. You can also experiment with other common stitches, such as daisy, herringbone, and even simple running stitch.

SWISS DARNING ON VERTICAL ROWS

Bring needle out on right side of knitting under strand at the bottom of a knit stitch (base of V-shape). Insert needle from right to left behind knit stitch directly above and pull the yarn snug. Insert needle under same strand where the thread emerged for first half-stitch. Bring needle out under the connecting strand of the knit stitch directly above it.

SWISS DARNING ON HORIZONTAL ROWS

Bring the needle up on the right side under the connecting thread at the bottom of a knit stitch. Insert needle from right to left behind the knit stitch above, and pull the yarn snug. Insert needle under the same strand where thread emerged for the first half stitch. Bring needle up again under the connecting strand of the stitch to the left of it.

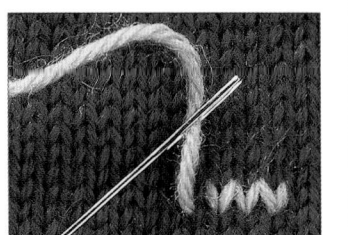

COUCHING

This is a way to secure one or several strands of yarn to your fabric. First lay your yarn across the fabric. Taking a different yarn on a needle, bring the needle to the front where you want the couching to begin. Make small evenly spaced stitches over the couched yarn; fasten off. Take the couched yarn to the back of the work and secure.

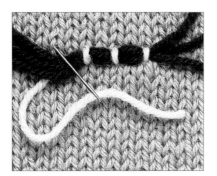

CROSS STITCH

Bring the yarn out at the front of the work at the bottom of a knit stitch, and take a diagonal stitch up to the right. Bring the needle out directly below, and pull the yarn snug. To complete the cross, insert the needle directly above where it first emerged. If making a 2nd cross stitch, bring it out at the bottom to the left and continue as in step 1.

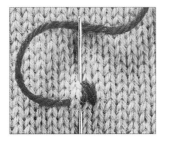

BULLION KNOT

Similar to a French knot, this stitch may be worked singly or in clusters. Bring the yarn out at the front of the work at the position for the knot. Make a backstitch the size of the knot(s) required, bringing the needle out at the front next to the first stitch. Twist the yarn around the needle point as many times as required to equal the backstitch length. Hold your left thumb on the coiled yarn and pull the needle through the coils. Then turn the needle back to where it was first inserted, and pull the yarn through to the back of the work so that the bullion knot lies flat.

CHAIN STITCH

Bring the needle through to the front. Form the yarn into a loop and, holding the loop in place, insert the needle back through the same hole. Hold the loop and bring the needle back to the front a stitch length away. With the yarn under the needle, pull the needle through to make the first chain. Insert the needle beside the emerging yarn, then bring to the front a stitch away, pulling the needle over the yarn to make a chain. Continue in this way.

SQUARED FILLING STITCH

Work a series of long, equally sized horizontal stitches at even intervals. Work long vertical stitches across these, at even intervals, to make the framework. Make small diagonal stitches at each point where the vertical yarns cross the horizontal.

STEM STITCH

Work from left to right, taking regular, slanted backstitches. The yarn should always emerge on the left of the previous stitch.

EMBROIDERED PILLOW

This pretty pillow has a knitted cover in two blocks of blue and lavender. Beautiful embroidery and colorful pompoms give it an extra decorative pop.

❖ **SIZE**
One size: 18" (46 cm) square

❖ **MATERIALS**
Yarn Sport weight 50% merino wool/50% cotton (approx 123 yds/113 m per 50 g ball). 4 x 50 g balls Color A (navy), 1 x 50 g ball Color B (lavender), plus small amounts of red and yellow for embroidery and pompoms
Needles One pair each No. 2 (2.75 mm) and No. 4 (3.25 mm) or size to obtain gauge
Notions Tapestry needle, 5 buttons, 18" (46 cm) square pillow form

❖ **GAUGE**
24 sts and 32 rows = 4" (10 cm) over stockinette stitch

❖ **SKILLS USED**
Stockinette st (p12), seams (p27), twisted rib st (p30), embroidery (p56), changing color (p60), eyelets (p89)

See pages 10–19 for knitting terms.

EMBROIDERED PILLOW

FRONT

With No. 4 needles cast on 54 sts in Color B and then 54 sts in Color A—108 sts. Work 9" (23 cm) in st st, twisting Colors A and B around each other at center point to avoid holes (see page 61).

Swap colors so that Color A is on top of Color B and vice versa. Work 9" (23 cm) in st st as before, then bind off.

BACK

(made in 2 sections)

Section 1: (Button band)

With Color A and No. 4 needles cast on 108 sts. Work 8½" (21.5 cm) in st st. Change to No. 2 needles and work 1" (2.5 cm) in twisted rib (K1b, P1). Bind off in rib. Place markers for 5 buttons equally spaced along center of button band.

Section 2: (Buttonhole band)

Work as for section 1 until rib measures ½" (1 cm). Make 5 open eyelets (see page 89) as buttonholes to correspond with markers. Cont in twisted rib until buttonhole band measures 1" (2.5 cm) and then bind off.

FINISHING

Block pillow front and back to measurements. Embroider pillow front following chart. With RS facing, join back sections 1 and 2 at side edges of twisted rib, placing buttonhole band (section 2) on top of button band (section 1). Sew pillow back and front together on inside along four seams. Press seams. Attach 5 buttons beneath buttonholes. Make 4 multicolored pompoms (see page 37) and attach to corners. Insert pillow form.

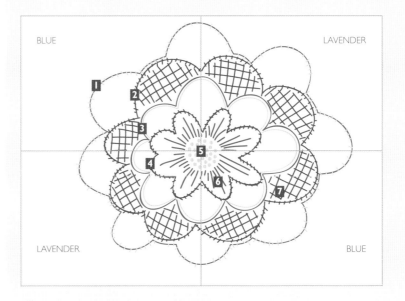

EMBROIDERING THE PILLOW

Enlarge this chart on a photocopier by approximately 400 per cent, to the right size to fit the pillow front. Trace off the four flower shapes that make up the pattern and cut each one out. Lay each one on the pillow cover in turn, basting around the outside of each to transfer the pattern to the cover. Following the basting lines and using the chart as a guide, embroider the pattern. Instructions for embroidery on knitting can be found on pages 56–57.

1 Work chain stitch around the outside of the pattern in red. Thread yellow yarn in and out of the chain stitch.

2 Work stem stitch around the outside of the second flower shape. Use the blue yarn over the lavender squares, and the lavender over the blue.

3 Work chain stitch in red round the third flower and then another line of chain stitch in yellow.

4 Using blue yarn, work couching around the fourth flower.

5 Work a cluster of bullion knots at the center.

6 Make straight stitches of varying lengths, radiating out from the center.

7 Fill the second flower shape with squared filling stitch. Use the blue yarn over the lavender squares, and the lavender over the blue.

CHANGING COLOR

Color is another way to transform your knitting. Its use may be subtle or dramatic, providing a mosaic of shades in a complex arrangement.

The simplest way to vary color is to make horizontal stripes; you introduce a new shade at the beginning of a row. To make vertical stripes, use a separate ball of yarn for each color. When you get to the end of each block, pick up the new yarn in a way that prevents a hole from appearing (see page 61). Another effective but easy way of adding color is to combine two different yarns, working them together as one strand. Color also may be embroidered onto a stockinette stitch background (see pages 56–57).

Simple color patterns in knitting, called intarsia, are often shown in chart form. Charts can be colored or printed in black and white with symbols representing the different colors.

The key to successful working with color is to organize your different yarns correctly and to keep your work neat. It's also important to keep the stitch gauge even, especially when changing colors within a row.

BOBBINS

When working with many different colors or when only small amounts of yarn are needed, use plastic or cardboard bobbins to help keep your work neat. If you choose cardboard, make a slit in the top to catch the yarn. If only a small amount of a color is needed, cut a short length of yarn for that part of the design.

Bring a burst of color to your knitting and try out a pretty patterned garment like this daisy tunic (see page 72).

ADDING NEW YARN AT THE START OF A ROW

Use this method when knitting horizontal stripes. If you will be using the old color again, leave it at the side. Make sure any ends are woven neatly into the edge or back of the work.

1 *Insert your right-hand needle into the first stitch on your left-hand needle and wrap both the old and new yarns over it. Knit the stitch with both yarns.*

2 *Drop the old yarn and pick up the short end of the new yarn and knit the next two stitches with the short end and the working yarn.*

3 *Drop the short end of the new yarn and continue knitting in pattern. On the subsequent row, knit the three double stitches in the ordinary way.*

ADDING NEW YARN AND WEAVING IN

When joining a color on the wrong side at the start of a row, use this method to weave the ends of yarns into the work.

1 *Cut the old color, leaving about 3 inches (7.5 cm). With the new yarn, purl the first two stitches. Lay the short ends of both the old and new yarns over the top of the needle and purl the next stitch under the short ends.*

2 *Leave the short ends hanging and purl the next stitch over them. Continue purling under and over the short ends until they are woven in.*

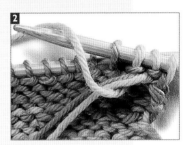

MAKING VERTICAL STRIPES OR DESIGNS

This method is known as intarsia and is suitable for knitting motifs. The pattern instructions are always in chart form. To make vertical stripes or independent blocks of color, use a separate ball or bobbin of yarn for each color. Drop the old yarn and pick up the next one from underneath it so the yarns cross. By twisting the yarns in this way, you will prevent a gap appearing in the work. Work in the same way for the purl row.

WORKING FROM A CHART

Color patterns are often charted on graph paper. Each square represents a stitch and each horizontal line of squares is a row of stitches. A colored-in chart (far right), where the indicated colors fill the graphed squares, is the easiest to follow and has the added advantage of giving you a preview of what the finished work will look like.

Many knitting charts are printed in black and white and indicate colors with different symbols (right). These charts usually come with a color key, and show only one pattern repeat. In the case of a multicolored sweater, the chart may represent the whole garment.

Charts are read from bottom to top; they are usually based on stockinette stitch where the first and all odd-numbered rows are knitted from right to left and all even-numbered rows are purled from left to right. Therefore, the first stitch of a chart is the bottom one on the right. You may find placing a ruler under each row will help you keep track of where you are. When knitting in the round (see pages 76–77), the right side always faces you so that you always read every row of the chart from right to left.

30 sts

30 sts

△ GREEN

+ YELLOW

• BLUE

☐ BEIGE

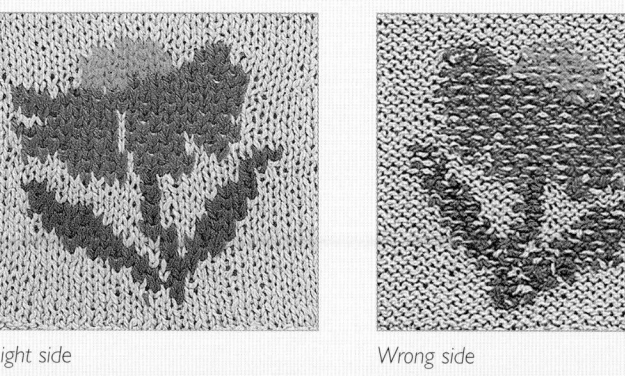

Right side *Wrong side*

ADDING NEW YARN WITHIN THE ROW

Use this method when using the original yarn again in the same row. The yarn not in use has to be carried along the back of the work. Use stranding over short distances (five stitches or less) and weaving when the yarn is carried along six stitches or more.

1 *Leaving the old yarn in the back of your work, insert your right-hand needle into the stitch. Wrap the new yarn over the needle and use this to knit the stitch.*

2 *Knit the next two stitches with the doubled length of new yarn.*

3 *Drop the short end and continue knitting with the new yarn while carrying the old yarn across the back. On subsequent rows, knit the double stitches normally.*

STRANDING

When a color is used again, the yarn, known as a float, is picked up and carried across the back of the work to make the new stitch. The float should be carried across at the same tension as your knitting and cross no more than five stitches.

WEAVING

In this method, the carried yarn is brought alternately above and below each stitch made so that it is woven in as you go. It is best worked using both hands. If knitting with many different colors, use small lengths of yarn wound around bobbins or cards.

YARN ABOVE THE STITCH

Holding one yarn in each hand, k1 (left) or p1 (right) with the first color, and, at the same time, bring the second color over the tip of your right-hand needle.

YARN BELOW THE STITCH

With one yarn in each hand, k1 (left) or p1 (right) with the first color, holding the second color below the first.

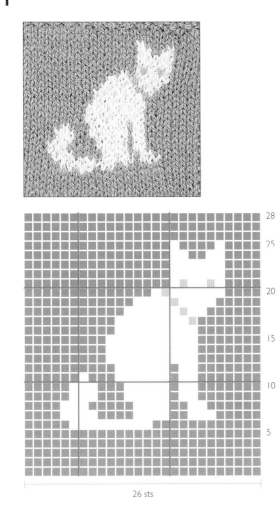

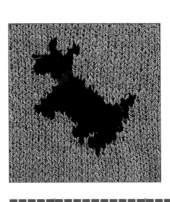

26 sts

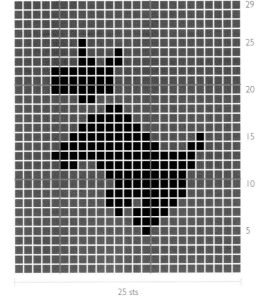

25 sts

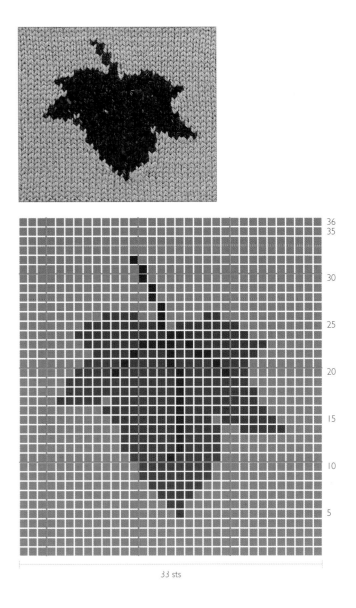

33 sts

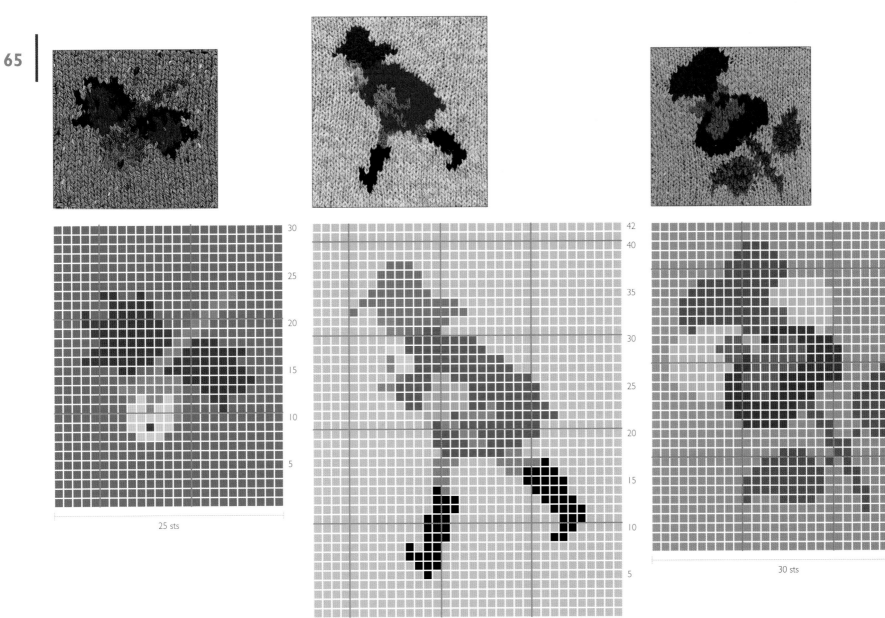

25 sts

34 sts

30 sts

CANDY-STRIPE LEG WARMERS

Great for keeping warm during dance or exercise class, leg warmers are also back as a fashion accessory. These are knitted as one piece on plain needles then made into a cylinder with a side seam. The twisted rib ends help them cling to your legs. Each leg warmer is knitted in a different colorway, but you could make both the same.

❖ **SIZES**
One size: To fit average leg, finished size 19" x 11" circumference (48 x 27 cm)

❖ **MATERIALS**
Yarn Knitting worsted 100% merino wool (131 yds/120 m per 50 g) 2 x 50 g balls Color A, 2 x 50 g balls Color B
Needles One pair each No. 5 (3.75 mm) and No. 6 (4 mm) or sizes to obtain gauge
Notions Tapestry needle

❖ **GAUGE**
22 sts and 30 rows = 4" (10 cm) over stockinette stitch using No. 6 needles

❖ **SKILLS USED**
Stockinette st (p12), seams (p27), twisted rib st (p30), changing color (p60),

See pages 10–19 for knitting terms.

BLUE LEG WARMER

With Color B and No. 5 needles cast on 60 sts.

Work 20 rows in twisted rib (K1b, p1) in stripe sequence:

2 rows Color B

4 rows Color A

Work a further 2 rows Color B.

Change to No. 6 needles and Color A and work in st st until piece measures 16" (41 cm) from cast-on edge. Cont with No. 6 needles and repeat stripe sequence in twisted rib.

Bind off in twisted rib with yarn B.

PINK LEG WARMER

Work as for blue one reversing colors.

FINISHING

Block and press pieces on wrong side. Join seams with a back stitch.

HOT STRIPES TOTE

Pack up your knitting in this handy, roomy bag. Stitched in the simplest garter stitch, it's so easy to make. The clever combination of pinks, reds, purples, and orange makes this bag really stand out.

✤ SIZES
11" x 11½" (28 x 29 cm)

✤ MATERIALS
Yarn *Sport weight 100% cotton (approx 126 yds/115 m per 50 g). 1 x 50 g ball each Color A, Color B, Color C, Color D, Color E, Color F*
Needles *One pair No. 5 (3.75 mm) or size to obtain gauge*
Notions *Tapestry needle*

✤ GAUGE
24 sts and 36 rows = 4" (10 cm) in striped pattern

✤ SKILLS USED
Garter st (p10), seams (p27), changing color (p60), twisted cord (p69)

See pages 18–19 for knitting terms.

HOT STRIPES TOTE
BAG BACK

Cast on 66 sts using Color E. Work 104 rows in stripe pattern as follows:
2 rows garter st Color E.
2 rows garter st Color A.
2 rows garter st Color E.
6 rows st st Color D.
2 rows garter st Color C.
4 rows st st Color D.
2 rows each garter st Colors B, F, D, F, B respectively.
4 rows st st Color C.
2 rows st st Color D.
6 rows st st Color C.
2 rows garter st Color A.
2 rows garter st Color E.
2 rows garter st Color A.
6 rows st st Color D.
2 rows garter st Color C.
4 rows st st Color D.
2 rows each garter st Colors F, B, C, B, F respectively.
4 rows st st Color C.
2 rows st st Color D.
6 rows st st Color C.
2 rows garter st Color E.
2 rows garter st Color A.
2 rows garter st Color E.
6 rows st st Color D.
2 rows garter st Color C.
4 rows st st Color D.
2 rows each garter st Colors B, F, B respectively.
Bind off in Color B.

BAG FRONT

Work the same as for back.

FINISHING

Put the front and back RS tog and oversew the sides and the base. Turn to RS. Make two 40" (102 cm) twisted cords (see below) using Colors C and D. Stitch the cords to the sides of the bag and knot at the base. Steam lightly. Tie the straps together at your required length.

MAKING A TWISTED CORD

The thicker the cord you want, the more strands of yarn you will need. The minimum is four strands. The length of the strands should be three times the length of the finished cord, including the tassel. Tie the strands together at one end and loop over a door handle, then stand back and hold the yarn taut in one hand. Twist the strands toward the right until a firm twist has been obtained along the whole length of the strands. Still holding the yarn taut, remove the strands from the door handle, and fold in half lengthways. Knot together the two ends about 1–1½" (2.5–3.75 cm) from the end. Hold the knotted end and let the cord twist up on itself, then smooth out any irregularities. Snip the yarns at the end to form a tassel.

BIG LOVE THROW

Have a heart and make someone you love this gorgeous throw—if you can bear to part with it, that is! It's made up of knitted squares, half worked in one colorway and half worked in another, each with a plump heart at its center. Hot, bright colors have been used here, but pick shades that match your home and mood.

❖ SIZE
One size: 48" wide and 70" long, (122 x 178 cm), excluding tassels

❖ MATERIALS
Yarn *Sport weight 70% lambswool/26% kid mohair/4% nylon (approx 153 yds/140 m per 50 g ball). 8 x 50 g balls each Color A and Color C, 11 x 50 g balls Color B*
Needles *One pair No. 8 (5 mm) or size to obtain gauge*
Notions *Tapestry needle*

❖ GAUGE
24 sts and 32 rows = 4" (10 cm) over intarsia design

❖ SKILLS USED
Stockinette st (p12), seams (p27), moss st (p31), changing color (p60)

See pages 18–19 for knitting terms.

56

50

40

30

20

10

51 sts

BIG LOVE THROW

Use separate balls of yarn for moss st at right and left of heart motif. Use one ball of yarn for heart and weave background along behind motif.

BASIC SQUARE

For colorway 1: With color A cast on 51 sts. Follow graph up to row 56, working the border color in moss st (see page 31) and the heart panel in st st. Bind off. Make 30 squares in colorway 1 and 30 squares in colorway 2.

FINISHING

Join squares together with a back stitch following chart (right) for background color and orientation. Tidy loose ends back into own colors. Press on right side with a warm iron over a damp cloth.
Make 7 10" (25 cm) fringe tassels (see page 35) and fasten to top and bottom of throw at outside edges and at seams of squares. Steam tassels.

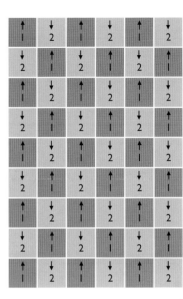

	Colorway 1	Colorway 2
Border	A	B
Background	B	C
Heart	C	A

- ■ Color A
- ■ Color B
- ■ Color C

DAISY TUNIC

This pretty sweater is decorated with bold floral motifs and striped sleeves in matching colors. It's mostly worked in stockinette stitch—just follow the chart to create the flower designs.

❖ **SIZES**
XS, S, M, L, XL: To fit bust 32 (34, 36, 38, 40)" (81 [86, 91.5, 96.5, 101.5] cm). Finished size: Bust 36 (38, 40, 42, 44)" (91.5 [96.5, 101.5, 106.5, 112] cm)

❖ **MATERIALS**
Yarn Lightweight 100% cotton (approx 126 yds/115 m per 50 g ball). 6 (7, 7, 8, 9) x 50 g balls Color A, 2 x 50 g balls each Colors B, C & D
Needles One pair each No. 4 (3.25 mm) and No. 6 (4 mm), one circular No. 4 (3.25 mm), or size to obtain gauge
Notions Tapestry needle, stitch holder

❖ **GAUGE**
22 sts and 26 rows = 4" (10 cm) over intarsia and stripe patterns

❖ **SKILLS USED**
Stockinette st (p12), increasing (p20), decreasing (p22), seams (p27), moss st (p31), changing color (p60), knitting in the round (p76), picking up sts (p88)

See pages 18–19 for knitting terms and page 94 for measurement chart.

DAISY TUNIC
BACK

With Color A and No. 4 needles cast on 100 (104, 110, 116, 122) sts.

Work 6 (6, 6, 8, 8) rows moss st (see page 31).

Change to No. 6 needles and, working in st st, work the last 14 (16, 1, 4, 7) sts of chart, then work all the 36 sts of chart 2 (2, 3, 3, 3) times, then work the first 14 (16, 1, 4, 7) sts. Continue in this way, repeating the 54 rows of chart until piece measures 17" (43 cm) from cast on edge ending on WS row.

SHAPE RAGLAN ARMHOLE

Bind off 5 sts at beg of next 2 rows—90 (94, 100, 106, 112) sts. ***Keeping patt correct as set, dec 1 st at both ends of next and every row 4 (8, 12, 16, 18) times, then every alt row 20 (18, 17, 15, 16) times—42 (42, 42, 44, 44) sts.

SHAPE BACK NECK

Next row (RS): K2tog, k5 and turn, leaving rem sts on holder. Work each side of neck separately.

Bind off 4 sts at beg of next row.

Next row (RS): K2tog and bind off last st. With RS facing rejoin yarn to rem sts. Bind off center 28 (28, 28, 30, 30) sts, work to last 2 sts, k2tog. Work to match first side, reversing shapings.

FRONT

Work as for back to ***

Keeping patt correct as set, dec 1 st at both ends of next and every row 4 (8, 12, 16, 18) times, then every alt row 16 (14, 13, 11, 12) times—50 (50, 50, 52, 52) sts.

SHAPE FRONT NECK

Next row (RS): K2tog, k17 and turn, leaving remaining sts on a holder. Work each side of neck separately.

Bind off 5 sts at beg of next row—14 sts. Dec 1 st at neck edge on next 4 rows. At the same time dec 1 st at raglan edge on next and foll alt row—8 sts.

Dec 1 st at both ends of next and foll 2 alt rows—2 sts.

Next row (WS): P2 tog and bind off. With RS facing, rejoin yarn to rem sts. Bind off center 12 (12,12, 14, 14) sts, work to last 2 sts, k2tog. Work to match first side, reversing shapings.

LEFT SLEEVE

With Color A and No. 4 needles cast on 49 (49, 53, 53, 53) sts and work 8 rows moss st.

Change to No. 6 needles and work in st st, repeating stripe sequence to end:

4 rows Color D, 4 rows Color C, 4 rows Color A.

At the same time inc 1 st at both ends of every 9th row 0 (6, 0, 0, 6) times, then every 10th row 6 (5, 0, 6, 5) times, then every 11th row 4 (0, 4, 4, 0) times, then every 12th row 0 (0, 5, 0, 0) times—69 (71, 71, 73, 75) sts. Continue even until sleeve measures 18½" (47 cm) from cast on edge ending with a WS row.

SHAPE RAGLAN

Bind off 5 sts at beg of next 2 rows. Keeping patt correct as set, dec 1 st at both ends of next and every alt row 12 (15, 13, 16, 15) times, then every 3rd row 8 (6, 8, 6, 8) times—19 sts. End with a RS row. **

SHAPE NECK

Bind off 6 sts at beg of next row, then dec 1 st at beg of foll row, rep last 2 rows once more. Work 1 row. Bind off rem 5 sts.

RIGHT SLEEVE

Work as for left sleeve to **. Work 1 row ending with a WS row.

SHAPE NECK

Bind off 6 sts at beg and dec 1 st at end of next row. Work 1 row, rep last 2 rows once more. Bind off rem 5 sts.

FINISHING

Join raglan sleeves onto back and front.

NECKBAND

With Color A and circular needle and RS facing pick up and knit 18 sts at top of left sleeve, 36 (36, 36, 38, 38) sts at front neck, 18 sts at right sleeve and 36 (36, 36, 38, 38) sts from back neck—108 (108, 108, 112, 112) sts. Work 6 rounds moss st. Bind off loosely in moss st.

Join sleeve seams and side seams. Steam lightly.

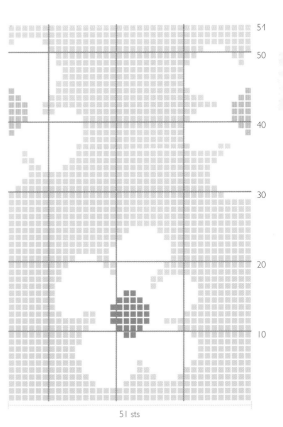

51 sts

BANDED SILK WRAP

This soft and appealing top wraps around the body to keep you warm in style. It's knitted in a luxurious silver-gray silk yarn, and trimmed with a contrasting sugary pink—although you can choose any two colors that you like.

❖ **SIZE**
XS, S, M, L, XL: To fit bust 32 (34, 36, 38, 40)" (81 [86, 91.5, 96.5, 101.5] cm). Finished size: Bust 33 (35, 37, 39, 41)" (84 [89, 94, 99, 104] cm)

❖ **MATERIALS**
Yarn Sport weight 100% pure silk (203 yds/186 m per 50 g). 5 (5, 6, 6, 7) x 50 g balls Color A, 1 x 50 g ball Color B
Needles One pair each No. 2 (2.75 mm) and No. 3 (3 mm) or size to obtain gauge
Notions Tapestry needle, stitch holder

❖ **GAUGE**
28 sts and 38 rows = 4" (10 cm) over stockinette stitch

❖ **SKILLS USED**
Stockinette st (p12), increasing (p20), decreasing (p22), seams (p27), moss st (p31), changing color (p60), picking up sts (p88)

See pages 18–19 for knitting terms and page 94 for measurement chart.

BANDED SILK WRAP

BACK

INCREASE ROWS

RS rows: K2, M1 (see page 21), k to last 2 sts, M1, k2.

WS rows: P2, M1, p to last 2 sts, M1, p2.

Using No. 2 needles and Color B cast on 102 (106, 112, 118, 124) sts and work 1¼" (3 cm) in moss st (see page 31). Change to Color A and No. 3 needles and working in st st, cont until work measures 7½ (7¾, 7½, 7¾, 7½)" (19 [19.5, 19, 19.5, 19.5] cm) from cast on edge ending on WS row. At the same time, inc 1 st as above at both ends of first and then every foll 6th row 0 (0, 0, 0, 7) times, every 7th row 0 (4, 0, 6, 2) times, every 8th row 4 (3, 7, 2, 0) times, every 9th row 2 (0, 0, 0, 0) times—116 (122, 128, 136, 144) sts.

ARMHOLE SHAPING

Bind off 6 (6, 7, 7, 7) sts at beg of next 2 rows. Dec 1 st at both ends of next and every alt rows 2 (5, 6, 10, 13) times, then cont as set until work measures 14½ (14¾, 15, 15¼, 15½)" (37 [37.5, 38, 38.5, 39] cm) from cast on edge ending on WS row— 100 (100, 102, 102, 104) sts.

NECK AND SHOULDER SHAPING

Work each side of neck separately. Work 32 (31, 32, 31, 32) sts transfer rem 68 (69, 70, 71, 72) sts to holder, turn and p2, p2tog tbl (see page 23), then work to end. Turn, place 10 (9, 10, 9, 10) sts on holder, work to end. Turn, p2, p2tog tbl, work to end. Turn, place 10 (10, 10, 10, 10) sts on holder, work to end. Work 1 row. Bind off across all 30 (29, 30, 29, 30) sts. With RS facing, leave center 36 (38, 38, 40, 40) sts on holder, rejoin yarn to rem sts and work to end. Work to match first side, reversing shapings (ie: work to last 3 sts, p2tog, p2).

LEFT FRONT

DECREASE ROWS

RS rows: K to last 3 sts, k2tog, k2.

WS rows: P2, p2tog tbl, work to end.

Using No. 2 needles and Color B cast on 102 (106 , 112, 118, 124) sts and work 1¼" (3 cm) in moss st, ending on a WS row, then change to No. 3 needles and Color A and work in st st to end. At the same time, starting on row 2 of moss st, dec 1 st at neck edge on every row, as above, 14 (18, 22, 28, 32) times, then every alt row 57 (56, 55, 53, 52) times—30(29, 30, 29, 30) sts. At the same time, starting on first row of Color A, inc 1 st, as on back increase rows, at outside edge then every foll 6th row 0 (0, 0, 0, 7) times, every 7th row 0 (4, 0, 6, 2) times, every 8th row 4 (3, 7, 2, 0) times, every 9th row 2 (0, 0, 0, 0) times. When work measures 7½ (7¾, 7½, 7¾, 7½)" (19 [19.5, 19, 19.5, 19.5] cm) from cast on edge ending on WS row, shape armhole, maintaining shaping at neck edge: Bind off 6 (6, 7, 7, 7) sts at beg of next row. Work 1 row. Dec 1 st at beg of next and every alt rows 2 (5, 6, 10, 13) times. When all shaping is completed, continue even until work measures 14½ (14¾, 15, 15¼, 15½)" (37 [37.5, 38, 38.5, 39] cm) from cast on edge ending on WS row and then shape shoulder: Place 10 (9, 10, 9, 10) sts at beg of next row on holder, work to end. Work 1 row. Place 10 (10, 10, 10, 10) sts at beg of next row on holder, work to end. Work 1 row. Bind off across all 30 (29, 30, 29, 30) sts.

RIGHT FRONT

DECREASES

RS rows: K2, k2tog tbl (see page 23), k to end.

WS rows: P to last 3 sts, p2tog, p2.

Work as left front reversing all shapings, working decs at neck edge as above.

SLEEVES

Using No. 2 needles and Color B cast on 58 (60, 62, 64, 64) sts and work 1¼" (3 cm) in moss st. Change to Color A and No. 3 needles and working in st st, to end, inc 1 st, as on back increase rows, at both ends of every 9th row 8 (8, 8, 8, 16) times, then every 10th row 7 (7, 7, 7, 0) times— 88 (90, 92, 94, 96) sts. Cont as set until work measures 17¾ (17½, 17¾, 18, 18)" (45 [44.5, 45, 45.5, 45.5] cm) from cast on edge and then shape sleeve cap: Bind off 6 (6, 7, 7, 7) sts at beg of next 2 rows. Following decrease rows for Left Front at left side and for Right Front and right side, dec 1 st at both ends of next and every alt row 17 (15, 13, 11, 14) times, then every 3rd row 5 (7, 9, 11, 9) times—32 (34, 34, 36, 36) sts. Bind off 3 sts at beg of next 4 rows. Bind off rem 20 (22, 22, 24, 24) sts.

FINISHING

Join shoulder seams. Insert sleeves, placing any fullness evenly over sleeve cap. Join side and sleeve seams in one line leaving a 1" (2.5 cm) slit in right side seam above welt to accommodate tie.

NECKBAND AND TIES

Using No. 2 needles and Color B, cast on 210 (210, 240, 240, 254) sts, then with right side facing, pick up and knit 142 (144, 148, 150, 152) sts (1 st for each row) from right front neck edge to shoulder, 3 sts down back neck edge and 18 (19, 19, 20, 20) sts from holder at center back— 373 (376, 410, 413, 429) sts. Work 5 rows in moss st and then bind off in moss st. Work other side similarly, starting at center back, casting on the sts for tie at end. Join band neatly at center back on inside.

KNITTING IN THE ROUND

Knitting in the round is done on circular or double-pointed needles. Since the knitting is worked as a continuous spiral there are no seams to sew up, and a stronger garment is produced.

SPECIAL EQUIPMENT

Circular needles come in a range of lengths and sizes. The shortest are best for knitting collars or neckbands; long ones can be used for knitting large straight pieces. To mark the end of a round, colored markers are useful. Double-pointed needles come in sets of four or more, and in different lengths and sizes.

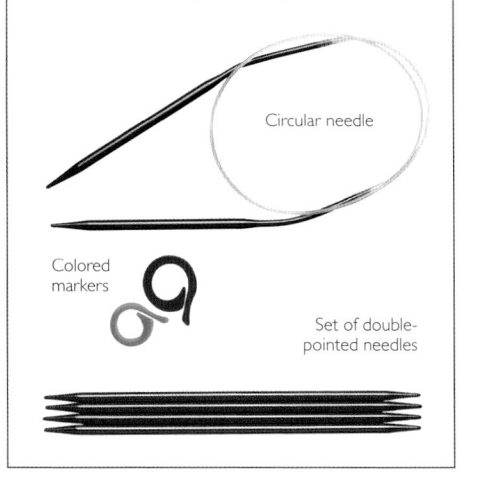

Circular needle

Colored markers

Set of double-pointed needles

Another advantage of knitting in the round is that the right side of the work is always facing you, so if you are working a color pattern you can see it clearly at all times. Stockinette stitch is simplified because you knit every row or round. Purling every row in the round produces reverse stockinette stitch.

There are two main ways of working in the round: with a flexible circular needle or with four or more double-pointed straight needles. A circular needle can hold three times as many stitches as a straight needle so it is the best way of knitting large items such as skirts. Small items such as socks, collars, and mittens are usually produced with four or more straight needles rather than a circular needle.

Knitting in the round may sound difficult, but these cozy slouch socks are a wonderfully easy way to start you off (see page 78).

USING A CIRCULAR NEEDLE

Choose a circular needle about 2 inches (5 cm) smaller than the circumference of the knitting to avoid stretching the stitches as you go. Work as if each pointed end is a separate needle.

1 *Cast on the number of stitches needed, then slip a marker between the first and last stitches so that you can see where the first round starts. Hold the needle tip with the last cast-on stitch in your right hand, and the tip with the first cast-on stitch in your left hand. At this point it is crucial to check for any twisted stitches by making sure the cast-on edge is facing the center of the needle. When knitting the first stitch of the round, pull the yarn firmly to avoid a gap.*

2 *Knit until you reach the marker, then slip the marker onto the right needle tip. You are now ready to start the second round.*

3 *Check again to see if any stitches are twisted. If so, ravel the first row—twisted stitches cannot be corrected in any other way—then continue in knit stitch.*

USING DOUBLE-POINTED NEEDLES

Usually these come in sets of four, but sometimes as many as six needles can be used. The working method is always the same: one needle is used to knit off the stitches that are equally divided between the other needles.

1 *Cast on one third of the stitches onto each of three needles. When you complete the stitches on one needle, hold the next one parallel and above it with the point a little bit further forward than the lower one.*

2 *Place the three needles in a triangle so the bottom edges of all stitches are facing the center. Place a marker after the last stitch, pulling the yarn through the marker.*

3 *Use the fourth needle to knit into the first cast-on stitch. Pull the yarn extra firmly on this stitch to avoid a gap in the work. When you have knitted all the stitches off the first needle, use it as the working needle to knit the stitches off the second needle, and so on.*

4 *Continue knitting in this way, holding the two working needles as you would normally, and dropping the needles not in use to the back of the work. When you reach the marker, slip it over and start the next round.*

SLOUCH SOCKS

These are socks to stay home in! Knitted in a chenille-style bulky cotton, they have a warm and soft texture. They are knitted on a set of double-pointed needles—working in the round is the perfect technique for socks.

❖ SIZES
One size: To fit average foot 10" (25.5 cm); leg 12" (30.5 cm)

❖ MATERIALS
Yarn Super Bulky Hand-dyed 100% cotton (109 yds/100 m per 100 g skein). 2 skeins
Needles One pair No. 8 (5 mm) set of five No. 6 (4 mm) dpn or sizes to obtain gauge
Notions Tapestry needle, stitch holder, stitch marker

❖ GAUGE
11 sts and 16 rows = 4" (10 cm) over stockinette stitch using No. 6 needles

❖ SKILLS USED
Stockinette st (p12), decreasing (p22), seams (p27), rib st (p30), knitting in the round (p76)

See pages 18–19 for knitting terms.

SLOUCH SOCKS

When working with random and hand-dyed yarns, disguise any difference in skein colors by using two skeins at a time. Work 2 rows from one skein and then 2 rows from the other, carrying the yarn not in use up the side of the work.

SOCKS

CUFF

With No. 8 needles cast on 26 sts loosely. Transfer the sts to 4 dpn, so that 6 sts are on the 1st, 7 sts on the 2nd, 6 sts on the 3rd and 7 sts on the 4th. Join into round, taking care not to twist the sts. Mark end of round with a marker, slipping the marker every round.
Work 2" (5 cm) in k1, p1 rib, then work in st st (k every round, see page 76) until piece measures 9½" (24 cm).

HEEL

*k1, k2tog; rep from * 3 more times, k1. Place these 9 sts onto holder. Work 16 rows back and forth in st st on rem 13 sts for heel. Bind off. Fold the bound off edge in half, WS together, and stitch together to form a short seam at the bottom of the heel. Turn right side out.

INSTEP

With RS facing, rejoin yarn at top of heel to left of held stitches. Pick up 8 sts along the left side of heel (every other row) and 1 st at seam. On another needle, pick up 8 sts along right edge of heel, place marker for beg of round. On a third needle, knit across 9 sts from holder—26 sts. Divide sts evenly on 4 needles, as before, and work in st st until foot measures 7" (17.75 cm), slipping the marker every round.

TOE

Round 1: Needle 1; sl 1 k-wise, psso, k to end. Needle 2; k to last 3 sts, k2tog, k1. Needle 3; sl 1 k-wise, psso, k to end. Needle 4; K to last 3 sts, k2tog, k1.
Rounds 2, 3 and 4: Work as for Round 1. Place rem 10 sts on two needles and graft together (see page 27).

FINISHING

Steam lightly to measurements. Attach 7" (17.75 cm) tassel (see page 35) to center back of each sock.

STRIPY FINGERLESS GLOVES

Snuggly and warm, these are great when you want to keep cozy but
need your fingers free, say for some knitting! They are made on
double-pointed needles, so you knit in a circle and
won't have any seams to sew together.

❖ SIZES
One size: To fit average hand, 7½" (19 cm) long

❖ MATERIALS
Yarn 4 ply wool (approx 162 yds/148 m per 25 g).
1 x 25 g ball each Color A, Color B, Color C, Color D,
Color E
Needles Set of four No. 2 (2.75 mm) dpn, set of four
No. 4 (3.25 mm) dpn or sizes to obtain gauge
Notions Stitch holders, stitch marker

❖ GAUGE
28 sts and 44 rows = 4" (10 cm) over stripe pattern
using the larger needles

❖ SKILLS USED
Garter st (p10), stockinette st (p12), increasing (p20),
decreasing (p22), twisted rib (p30), changing color (p60),
knitting in the round (p76), picking up sts (p88)

See pages 18–19 for knitting terms.

STRIPY FINGERLESS GLOVES

STRIPE PATTERN (24 ROW REPEAT)

4 rounds st st (k every round) Color B.
2 rounds garter st (k 1 round, p 1 round)
Color A.
4 rounds st st Color C.
2 rounds garter st Color A.
4 rounds st st Color D.
2 rounds garter st Color A.
4 rounds st st Color E.
2 rounds garter st Color A.

RIGHT GLOVE
CUFF

Using Color A and No. 2 dpn, cast on 48
stitches (16 on each of three needles). Join
into round, taking care not to twist the sts.
Mark end of round, slipping marker every
round.

Work 3" (7.5 cm) in twisted rib (K1b, p1).
Next round: Rib 2, inc in next st, *rib 4,
increase in next st, repeat from * to last 2
sts, rib 2 (60 sts).

Change to No. 4 dpn and work 18 rounds
in stripe pattern. Continue in pattern
correct as set.

**Round 19: Patt 30 sts, slip next 9 sts
onto a stitch holder and leave for thumb.
Cast on 9 stitches, patt to end.

Change to No. 2 dpn and cont in stripe
pattern until hand measures 4" (10 cm)
ending on first row of garter st in Color A.
Next round: Patt 34 sts, p2tog, patt to
end—59 sts.

FIRST FINGER

Using Color A, 1st needle k30 sts, 2nd
needle k8 sts, slip remaining 21 sts of
round and first 21 sts from 1st needle
onto holder. Cast on 3 sts—20 sts.
***Divide these 20 sts onto 3 needles.
Knit 5 rounds in Color A, purl 1 round in
Color A. Bind off loosely.

SECOND FINGER

With palm of glove facing, slip 7 sts from
holder onto needle. Using Color A, k7, cast

on 3 sts, k7, pick up and knit 3 sts from
base of first finger—20 sts.
Knit 5 rounds in Color A, purl 1 round in
Color A. Bind off loosely.

THIRD FINGER

As second, but sts picked up from base of
2nd finger.

FOURTH FINGER

Divide remaining 14 sts onto 2 needles
and using Color A knit them. Pick up and
knit up 3 sts from base of 3rd finger.
Knit 5 rounds in Color A, purl 1 round in
Color A. Bind off loosely.

THUMB

Using No. 4 dpn, slip 9 sts left on holder
onto needle, using 2nd needle pick up and
knit 9 sts from cast on sts. Divide sts onto
3 needles.
Knit 5 rounds in Color A, inc 4 sts evenly
across first row—22 sts. Purl 1 round in
Color A. Bind off loosely.

LEFT GLOVE

Work as for Right Glove until ** is
reached.
Round 19: Patt 21 sts, slip next 9 sts onto
holder for thumb, cast on 9 sts, patt to
end.

Change to set of No. 2 dpn and cont in
stripe pattern until hand measures 4" (10
cm) ending on first row of garter st in
Color A.

Next round: Patt 24 sts, p2tog, patt to
end—59 sts.

FIRST FINGER

Using Color A, 1st needle k29 sts, 2nd
needle k9 sts, slip remaining sts of round
and 21 sts from 1st needle onto a st
holder. Cast on 3 sts—20 sts.
Complete glove as for Right Hand reading
back of hand in place of palm and work
from *** to end.

FINISHING

Weave in any loose ends. Press lightly.

HOODIE SWEATER

Snuggly and warm, this hooded pullover uses two textured stitches to turn a simple garment into something more eye catching. Great for keeping cozy at home or to wear outdoors on a chilly day.

❖ SIZES

XS, S, M, L, XL: To fit bust 32(34, 36, 38, 40)" (81 [86, 9.5, 96.5, 101.5] cm). Finished size: Bust 38 (40, 43, 45, 47½)" (96 [101, 109, 114, 121] cm)

❖ MATERIALS

Yarn Bulky 60% wool/30% alpaca/10% acrylic (109 yds/100 m per 100 g). 9 (9, 10, 10, 11) x 100 g balls
Needles One pair No. 10½ (6.5 mm), one pair plus one extra No. 13 (9 mm), No. 10½ (6.5 mm) circular needle, or sizes to obtain gauge
Notions Tapestry needle, crochet hook

❖ GAUGE

14 sts and 18 rows = 4" (10 cm) over basketweave stitch

❖ SKILLS USED

Increasing (p20), decreasing (p22), seams (p27), moss st (p31), basketweave st (p32), knitting in the round (p76)

See pages 18–19 for knitting terms.

83

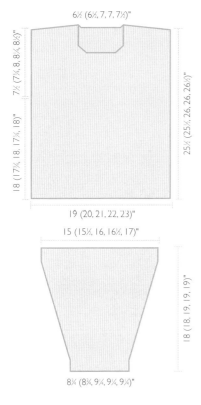

6½ (6¾, 7, 7, 7½)"

7½ (7¾, 8, 8¼, 8½)"

18 (17¾, 18, 17¾, 18)"

25½ (25½, 26, 26, 26½)"

19 (20, 21, 22, 23)"

15 (15½, 16, 16½, 17)"

18 (18, 19, 19, 19)"

8¾ (8¾, 9¼, 9¼, 9¼)"

HOODIE SWEATER
BACK
With No. 10½ needles, cast on 67 (71, 75, 79, 83) sts and work in moss st (see page 31) for 1" (2.5 cm). Change to No. 13 needles and work in basketweave st (see page 32) for 24 (24, 24.5, 24.5, 25)" (61[61, 62, 62, 63.5] cm), ending with a WS row. For sizes S and L, center patt by working extra 2 sts in patt at both ends on every row—i.e. Row 2 will read: P1, *k5, k3; rep from * to last 6 sts, k5, p1.

NECK AND SHOULDER SHAPING
Bind off 11 (12, 12, 13, 14) sts, patt next 13 (14, 15, 16, 16) sts; turn.
Next row: Bind off 2 sts, patt to the end. Bind off rem 11 (12, 13, 14, 14) sts.
Return to neck sts and bind off 19 (19, 21, 21, 23) sts, patt to end.
Next row: Bind off 11(12, 12, 13, 14) sts, patt to end.
Next row: Bind off 2 sts, patt to end. Bind off rem 11(12, 13, 14, 14) sts.

FRONT
Work as for back until front measures 21½ (21½, 22, 22, 22½)" (55[55, 56, 56, 57] cm).

NECK SHAPING
(RS) Patt 28 (30, 32, 33, 35) sts, bind off center 11 (11, 11, 13, 13) sts, patt 28 (30, 32, 33, 35) sts. Working on last 28 (30, 32, 33, 35) sts to end, patt 1 row.
*Bind off 2 sts at beg of next row then dec 1 st at neck edge on foll 4 (4, 5, 4, 5) alt rows. Cont until front measures the same as the back to shoulder, ending on WS row. Bind off 11 (12, 12, 13, 14) sts at beg of next row. Work 1 row. Bind off rem 11 (12, 13, 14, 14) sts.
Return to right side and work from *.

SLEEVE
With No. 10½ needles, cast on 35 (35, 37, 37, 37) sts. Work in moss st for 2" (5 cm).

Change to No. 13 needles. Cont in moss st to end, inc 1 st at both ends of next, and then every following 6th row 0 (0, 0, 2, 9) times—37 (37, 39, 43, 57) sts, then every 7th row 0 (9, 4, 8, 2) times—37 (55, 47, 59, 61) sts, then every 8th row 8 (0, 5, 0, 0) times—53 (55, 57, 59, 61) sts. Continue until sleeve measures 18 (18, 19, 19, 19)" (46 [46, 48, 48, 48] cm) from cast-on edge. Bind off.

HOOD
With No. 10½ circular needle, beg at left shoulder seam with RS facing, pick up and knit 21 sts down left neck, 13 (13, 13, 15, 15) sts across center front, 21 sts up right neck, and 23 (23, 25, 25, 27) sts across the back—78 (78, 80, 82, 84 sts).
Work in the round in moss st for 3" (7.5 cm). Carefully mark the center front stitch with a thread.
Next round: At center front, bind off 10 sts (5 sts each side of center). Cont around to last st before center front, k1. Cont working back and forth.
Next row: Slip 1 st knitwise, work 2 tog, work to the last st, k1.
Rep last round 10 times—57 (57, 59, 61, 63) sts.
Continue even, always knitting last stitch and slipping first stitch knitwise, until hood measures 9½" (24 cm) at center back.
Next row (RS): Patt 26 (26, 27, 28 ,29) sts, K2tog, k1, slip1, k1, psso, patt 26 (26, 27, 28, 29) sts.

Next row (WS): Patt to center 3 sts, p3, patt to end.
Continue in this way, decreasing each side of center stitch on right side rows until 33 (33, 35, 35, 37) sts remain. Now divide the stitches evenly onto two needles and with right sides facing, bind off using third needle to remove 2 sts simultaneously—one from each needle—pulling in the final odd stitch to make a smooth seam.

FINISHING
Join the shoulder seams (see page 27). With the center of the sleeve top at the shoulder seam, set in sleeve. Join sleeve and side seams. Steam lightly.

FRINGED PONCHO

This cozy poncho is perfect when you need an extra layer. It's made by combining two yarns that are worked together to give a rich texture. The shaped yoke and collar fit snugly around your shoulders.

❖ **SIZE**
One size: 40" wide and 24" long (101 x 61 cm)

❖ **MATERIALS**
Yarn Super bulky, 1 strand 100% viscose and 1 strand 78% mohair/13% wool/9% nylon worked together. Viscose (approx 109 yds/100 m per 100 g ball): 4 x 100 g balls. Mohair (approx 191 yds/175 m per 100 g ball): 3 x 100 g balls
Needles One pair each No. 10½ (6.5 mm) and No. 17 (12 mm), one No. 17 (12 mm) circular needle or sizes to obtain gauge
Notions Tapestry needle, crochet hook.

❖ **GAUGE**
7 sts and 10 rows = 4" (10 cm) over stockinette stitch using two strands held together, as above

❖ **SKILLS USED**
Garter st (p10), stockinette st (p12), increasing (p20), decreasing (p22), seams (p27), rib (p30), knitting in the round (p76), picking up sts (p88)

See pages 18–19 for knitting terms.

FRINGED PONCHO

Use a slip-stitch selvage (see page 14) to give a firm edge.

BACK

With 1 strand of viscose and 1 strand of mohair held together and No. 17 needles cast on 70 sts and work in st st until piece measures 18" (46 cm) from cast on edge, ending with WS row.

SHAPE NECK

Next row: K28 sts, bind off 14 sts, k28 sts. Work each side of neck separately.
Next row: Purl to last 2 sts, p2tog.
Next row: K2tog, knit to end of row.
Repeat last 2 rows once more. Bind off. Work other side of neck reversing shapings.

FRONT

Work as for back.

YOKE

The reverse side of the st st is the right side.
With knit sides together, join front and back shoulder seams.
Using 2 strands of mohair held together and circular needle, with RS facing, pick up and knit 58 sts evenly around neckline. Work 9" (23 cm) in K1, P1 rib. Bind off.

COLLAR

Using 2 strands of mohair held together and No. 10½ needles, with WS facing and starting at side, pick up and knit 58 sts from cast off edge at top of yoke. Work in garter st, inc 1 st at beg of each row until there are 73 sts. Bind off.

FINISHING

Make 82 5" (13 cm) tassels (see page 35) with mohair and attach to side edges of poncho, evenly spaced 1" (2.5 cm) apart. Steam lightly.

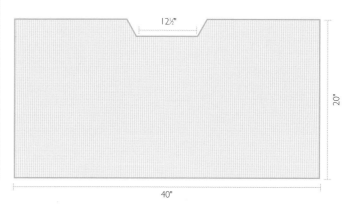

OPENWORK

Yarn-over increases form some of the loveliest and most delicate stitches a knitter can create. Made with fine yarns and needles, openwork patterns are ideal for gossamer shawls, lacy sweaters, or dressy scarves.

DOUBLE AND MULTIPLE INCREASES

Several stitches may be made by the yarn-over method. In stockinette stitch, to make a double increase (yo2) on a knit row, bring the yarn forward as for single yarn over (yo) but wrap it twice around the right needle before knitting the next stitch. On the next row, purl the first of the new stitches and knit the second.

When making multiple increases, yo3 (yo4, yo5, etc.), bring the yarn forward and then 3 (4, 5, etc.) times around the needle. On the next row, purl and knit the new stitches alternately, always knitting the last new stitch.

You can also use openwork patterns where a more robust appearance or a warmer fabric, is required, just use medium-weight yarn to knit patterns with smaller openings.

There are two major categories of openwork pattern—lace and eyelet. Lace is truly openwork, unlike eyelet which is solid work punctuated by small openings. Lace, when combined with other stitches, lends itself to being used as panels. Knit the panels in or near the center and away from the sides, where they are difficult to shape.

Wool, cottons, silks, and cashmere are among the many yarns that knit up beautifully in lace patterns. Cotton lace is often used for trimming curtains, place mats, bed linens, as well as clothes.

Try out some openwork techniques and create this shawl (see pages 92–93).

YARN OVER VISIBLE INCREASE

This increasing technique is used for lace and other fancy patterns as the method produces a hole, which forms an openwork pattern. The basic technique is to wind the yarn once around the needle to form a loop, which is knitted or purled on the next row. The yarn is wound in different ways depending on where the new stitch falls (see below). This yarn-over increase method is abbreviated as *yo*.

YARN OVER IN STOCKINETTE STITCH

To make a yarn over in stockinette stitch, bring the yarn forward to the front of the work, loop it over your right-hand needle [1] and knit the next stitch [2]. The loop and new stitch are on the right-hand needle [3]; knit to the end of the row. On the following row, and with the rest of the stitches, purl the loop in the usual way [4].

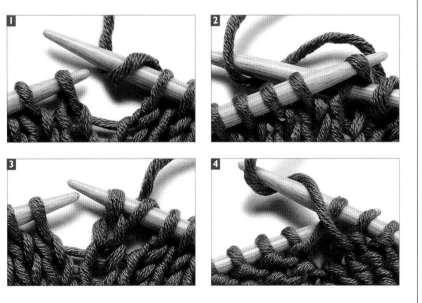

Between purl stitches in reverse stockinette stitch
Purl stitch, then take the yarn back over your right-hand needle then forward under it.

Between two knit stitches in garter stitch
Bring the yarn forward over your right-hand needle, then back under it again.

Between two purl stitches in garter stitch
Take the yarn to the back of the work and then bring it back over your right-hand needle to the front again.

Between knit and purl stitches in ribbing
After knitting a stitch, bring the yarn forward between your needles, then back over your right-hand needle and forward under it.

Between purl and knit stitches in ribbing
After purling, take the yarn over your right-hand needle from front to back.

OPENWORK BASICS

Openings are formed by yarn-over increases (see page 87), which are later offset by the same number of decreases so that the number of stitches remains constant. It is important that you work to the correct tension, and with appropriate needles and yarn. Openwork needs stretching before it is fully effective. Therefore, when you are substituting a lace pattern for stockinette stitch, cast on fewer stitches than the width requirement—about three-quarters the number should suffice.

EYELETS

There are two main types of eyelet: the chain and open. Made singly, eyelets can be used as tiny buttonholes or formed into a line for threading ribbon through. Used in combination, with plain rows between, eyelets can be placed vertically, horizontally, or diagonally to form decorative motifs. Do not make eyelets at the beginning or end of a row; work them at least two stitches in from the edge.

LACE EDGINGS

These are marvelous for trimming bed and table linens. Use fine crochet cotton and sew finished edging to the cloth. When trimming knitting with a lace edge, first complete the main piece then pick up the required number of stitches for the lace edge (below).

Picking up stitches for an edge
Hold the working yarn behind the completed piece and insert your knitting needle through it, between the rows and between the last two stitches of each row, from front to back. Take the yarn over the needle as if knitting and draw a loop of the yarn through to form a stitch. Continue until the correct number of stitches have been formed.

CHAIN EYELETS

This is the simplest and most common type of eyelet. It can be combined with the open eyelet in more intricate stitches. It is abbreviated as *yo, k2tog.*

1 *Make a yarn over by bringing your yarn to the front, and then knitting the next two stitches together.*

2 *The yarn over adds one stitch, but knitting two together reduces the stitches to the original number.*

3 *A chain eyelet has been made in the knitted work.*

OPEN EYELET

To work a slightly larger opening, use this method. This is more suitable for threading ribbon. It is abbreviated as *yo, sl* **1** *k-wise, k1, psso.*

1 *Make a yarn over by bringing the yarn forward around the front of your needle. Slip the next stitch knitwise, knit the next stitch, and then pass the slipped stitch over.*

2 *The increase made by the yarn over has been replaced by the slip-stitch decrease. The number of stitches remains the same.*

SLIP, SLIP, KNIT DECREASE

This decrease is especially useful for lace and openwork and leaves a smooth finish. It is abbreviated as ssk. Slip the first and second stitches knitwise, one at a time, onto your right-hand needle. Insert your left-hand needle into the fronts of these two stitches from the left, and knit them together from this position. The completed slip, slip, knit decrease is made.

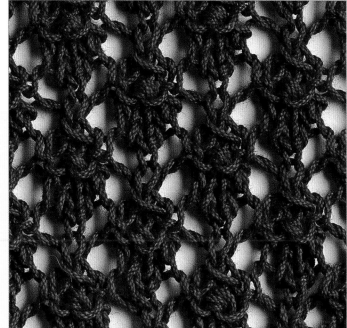

OPENWORK EYELETS

Multiple of 4 sts plus 3

Row 1 (right side): K.

Row 2: P.

Row 3: *K2, k2tog, yo; rep from * to last 3 sts, k3.

Row 4: P.

Row 5: K.

Row 6: P.

Row 7: *K2tog, yo, k2; rep from * to last 3 sts, k2tog, yf, k1.

Row 8: P.

Rows 1 to 8 form the pattern.

LATTICE STITCH

Multiple of 6 sts plus 1

Row 1 (right side): K1, *yo, p1, p3tog, p1, yo, k1; rep from * to end.

Row 2 and every alt row: P.

Row 3: K2, yo, sl 1, k2tog, psso, yo, *k3, yo, sl 1, k2tog, psso, yo; rep from * to last 2 sts, k2.

Row 5: P2tog, p1, yo, k1, yo, p1, *p3tog, p1, yo, k1, yo, p1; rep from * to last 2 sts, p2tog.

Row 7: K2tog, yo, k3, yo, *sl 1, k2tog, psso, yo, k3, yf; rep from * to last 2 sts, ssk.

Row 8: P.

Rows 1 to 8 form the pattern.

FLEURETTE

Multiple of 6 sts plus 5

Note: Sts should only be counted after rows 1-3, 6-9, and 12.

Row 1 and every alt row (wrong side): P.

Row 2: K2, *k1, yo, ssk, k1, k2tog, yo; rep from *, ending k3.

Row 4: K4, *yo, k3; rep from *, ending k1.

Row 6: K2, k2tog, *yo, ssk, k1, k2tog, yo, sl 2 k-wise, k1, p2sso; rep from *, ending yo, ssk, k1, k2tog, yo, ssk, k2.

Row 8: K2, *k1, k2tog, yo, k1, yo, ssk; rep from *, ending k3.

Row 10: As row 4.

Row 12: K2, *k1, k2tog, yo, sl 2 k-wise, k1, p2sso, yo, ssk; rep from *, ending k3.

Rows 1 to 12 form the pattern.

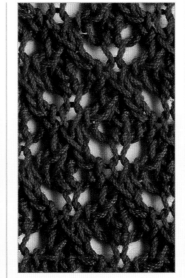

LEAF PATTERN

Multiple of 10 sts plus 1

Row 1 and every alt row (wrong side): P.

Row 2: K3, *k2tog, yo, k1, yo, ssk, k5; rep from *, ending last rep k3.

Row 4: K2, *k2tog, [k1, yo] twice, k1, ssk, k3; rep from *, ending last rep k2.

Row 6: K1, *k2tog, k2, yo, k1, yo, k2, ssk, k1; rep from * to end.

Row 8: K2tog, *k3, yo, k1, yo, k3, sl 1, k2tog, psso; rep from * to last 9 sts, k3, yo, k1, yo, k3, ssk.

Row 10: K1, *yo, ssk, k5, k2tog, yo, k1; rep from * to end.

Row 12: K1, *yo, k1, ssk, k3, k2tog, k1, yo, k1; rep from * to end.

Row 14: K1, *yo, k2, ssk, k1, k2tog, k2, yo, k1; rep from * to end.

Row 16: K1, *yo, k3, sl 1, k2tog, psso, k3, yo, k1; rep from * to end.

Rows 1 to 16 form the pattern.

ENGLISH LACE

Multiple of 6 sts plus 1

Row 1 and every alt row (wrong side): P.

Row 2: K1, *yo, ssk, k1, k2tog, yo, k1; rep from * to end.

Row 4: K1, *yo, k1 sl 1, k2tog, psso, k1, yo, k1; rep from * to end.

Row 6: K1, *k2tog, yo, k1, yo, ssk, k1; rep from * to end.

Row 8: K2tog, *[k1, yo] twice, k1, sl 1, k2tog, psso; rep from * to last 5 sts, [k1, yo] twice, k1, ssk.

Rows 1 to 8 form the pattern.

FALLING LEAVES

Worked over 16 sts on a background of reverse st st

Row 1 (right side): P1, k3, k2tog, k1, yo, p2, yo, k1, ssk, k3, p1.

Row 2 and every alt row: K1, p6, k2, p6, k1.

Row 3: P1, k2, k2tog, k1, yf, k1, p2, k1, yo, k1, ssk, k2, p1.

Row 5: P1, k1, k2tog, k1, yo, k2, p2, k2, yo, k1, ssk, k1, p1.

Row 7: P1, k2tog, k1, yo, k3, p2, k3, yo, k1, ssk, p1.

Row 8: K1, p6, k2, p6, k1.

Rows 1 to 8 form the pattern.

FEATHER PANEL

Worked over 13 sts on a background of reverse st st

Special abbreviation

S4K (Slip 4 knit): Slip next 4 sts knitwise, one at a time, onto right needle, then insert left needle into fronts of these 4 sts from left, and knit them together from this position.

Row 1 (right side): K.

Row 2: P.

Row 3: K4tog, [yo, k1] 5 times, yo, S4K.

Row 4: P.

Rows 1 to 4 form the pattern.

LACE SHAWL

This fine shawl owes its lacy appearance to an openwork stitch. Despite its delicate looks, it's cozy enough to keep you warm when you need that extra layer. Simple zigzag trimmings decorate the top and bottom edges and add the perfect finishing touch.

❖ SIZE
One size: 28" wide and 74" long (71 cm x 188 cm)

❖ MATERIALS
Yarn Sport weight 80% cashmere/20% extra fine merino (137 yds/125 m per 25 g). 22 x 25 g balls
Needles One pair each No. 1 (2.25 mm) and No. 3 (3 mm) or size to obtain gauge
Notions Tapestry needle, stitch holders

❖ GAUGE
26 sts and 34 rows = 4" (10 cm) over lozenge stitch

❖ SKILLS USED
Garter st (p10), seams (p27), openwork (p86), picking up sts (p88)

See pages *18–19* for knitting terms.

LACE SHAWL
LOZENGE ST
Multiple of 10sts +2

Row 1 (RS): K1,*yo, sl 1, k1 psso, k5, k2 tog, yo, k1, rep from * to last st, k1.

Row 2 and all even rows: Purl.

Row 3: K1, *k1, yo, sl 1, k1, psso, k3, k2tog, yo, k2, rep from * to last st, k1.

Row 5: K1, *k2, yo, sl 1, k1, psso, k1, k2tog, yo, k3, rep from * to last st, k1.

Row 7: K1, *k3, yo, sl 1, k2tog, psso, yo, k4, rep from * to last st, k1.

Row 9: K1, *k2, k2tog, yo, k1, yo, sl 1, k1, psso, k3, rep from * to last st, k1.

Row 11: K1, *k1, k2tog, yo, k3, yo, sl 1, k1, psso, k2, rep from * to last st, k1.

Row 13: K1, *k2tog, yo, k5, yo, sl 1, k1, psso, k1, rep from * to last st, k1.

Row 15: K1, * yo, k7, yo, sl 1, k2tog, psso, rep from * to end.

Rep rows 2—15.

With No. 3 needles cast on 182 sts and work 4 rows in garter st. Then work in lozenge st until work measures 72" (183 cm), ending on either row 7 or row 15. Work 4 rows in garter st. Bind off.

ZIGZAG TRIM
With No. 3 needles cast on 2 sts.

Row 1 (RS): K2.

Row 2: Yo, k2.

Row 3: Yo, k3.

Row 4: Yo, k4.

Row 5: Yo, k5.

Row 6: Yo, k6.

Row 7: Yo, k7.

Row 8: Yo, k8.

Row 9: Yo, k9 (10 sts).

Break yarn but leave the pointed shape on needle. On the same needle cast on 2 sts and work 2nd shape as first. Continue until 18 pointed shapes made. On last shape, do not break yarn but turn and knit across all shapes on the needle. Bind off. Repeat to make a second zigzag trim.

FINISHING
SIDE TRIMS
With No. 1 needles and RS facing, pick up and k1 st for each row along side edge of shawl. Work 4 rows garter st. Bind off. Sew zigzag trims to shawl at top and bottom (including side trims). Steam lightly.

DAISY TUNIC (page 72)

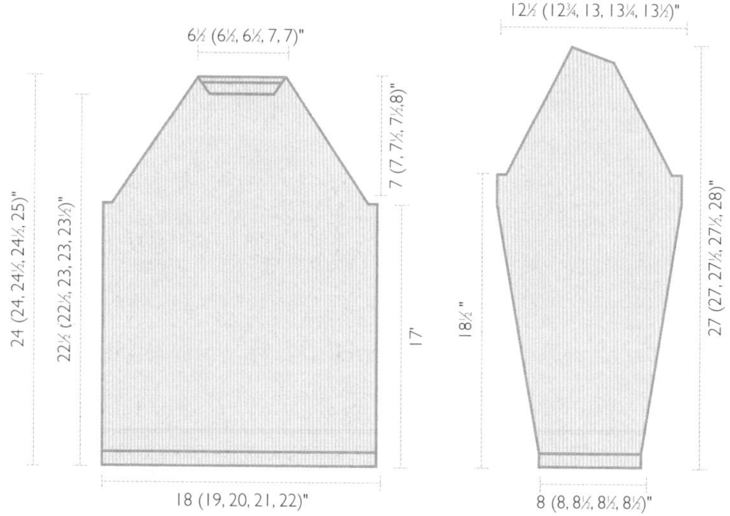
6½ (6½, 6½, 7, 7)"
24 (24, 24½, 24½, 25)"
22½ (22½, 23, 23, 23½)"
7 (7, 7½, 7½, 8)"
17"
18 (19, 20, 21, 22)"
12½ (12¾, 13, 13¼, 13½)"
18½ "
27 (27, 27½, 27½, 28)"
8 (8, 8½, 8½, 8½)"

BANDED SILK WRAP (page 74)

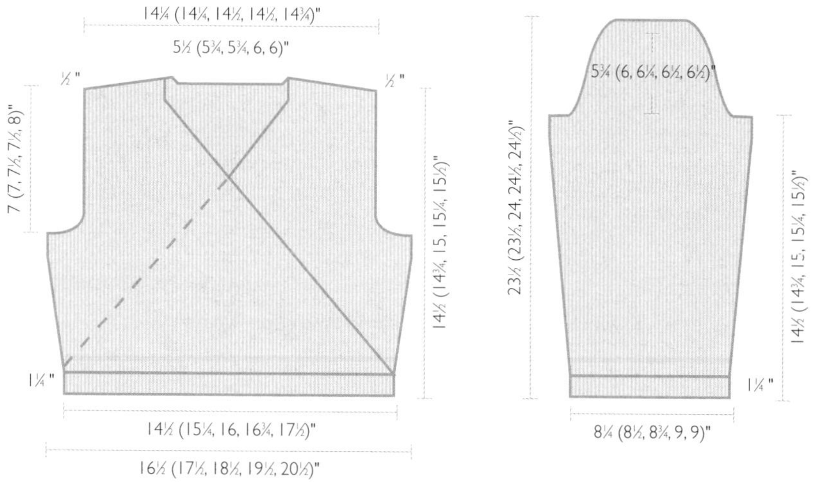
14¼ (14¼, 14½, 14½, 14¾)"
5½ (5¾, 5¾, 6, 6)"
½ "
½ "
7 (7, 7½, 7½, 8)"
14½ (14¾, 15, 15¼, 15½)"
1¼ "
14½ (15¼, 16, 16¾, 17½)"
16½ (17½, 18½, 19½, 20½)"
5¾ (6, 6¼, 6½, 6½)"
23½ (23¾, 24, 24½, 24½)"
14½ (14¾, 15, 15¼, 15½)"
1¼ "
8¼ (8½, 8¾, 9, 9)"

YARNS USED

Chunky scarf
Colinette Point 5
Alizarine #119

Mini bag
Rowan Cotton Glacé
Glee #799

Fringed top
Rowan Biggy Print
Color A Thunder #252
Color B Allsorts #255

Fringe benefits
Rowan Polar
Red Hot #641

Twisted rib hat
Rowan Big Wool
Color A Smitten Kitten #003
Color B Whoosh #014

Camisole
Colinette Giotto
Fresco #147

Flaps or no flaps?
Jaeger Matchmaker Merino
Hat with Flaps
Azalea #897
No Flaps
Fuchsia #887

Cotton cable backpack
Rowan Denim
Tennessee #231

Flirty sweater
Jaeger Albany
Peony #274

Embroidered pillow
Rowan Wool Cotton
Color A French navy #909
Color B August #953
Color C Rich #911
Color D Citron #901

Candy-stripe legwarmers
Jaeger Baby Merino DK
Color A Mallow #221
Color B Powder #222

Hot stripes tote
Rowan Cotton Glacé
Color A Candy Floss #747
Color B Glee #799
Color C Bubbles #724
Color D Spice #807
Color E Hyacinth #787
Color F Tickle #811

Big love throw
Rowan Kid Classic
Color A Pinched #819
Color B Juicy #827
Color C Cherish #833

Daisy tunic
Rowan Cotton Glacé
Color A Pier #809
Color B Hyacinth #787
Color C Tickle #811
Color D Bleached #726

Banded silk wrap
Jaeger Silk
Color A Silver Blue #131
Color B Brilliant #144

Slouch socks
Colinette Fandango
Ischia #131

Stripy fingerless gloves
Rowan Rowanspun 4 ply
Rowan Yorkshire Tweed 4 ply
Color A Whiskers #283
Color B Foxy #275
Color C Sugar #723
Color D Turkish #722
Color E Temptation #725

Hoodie sweater
Rowan Polar
Silver Lining #646

Fringed poncho
Colinette Mohair
Summer Berries #160
Colinette Isis
Earth #61

Lace shawl
Jaeger Cashmina
Blond #039

ACKNOWLEDGMENTS

Thank you to my good friend and fellow knitwear designer Jean Moss for sizing the patterns. To my dedicated hand knitters who worked on this book: Chriss Bebbington, Gwyneth Casewell, Yvonne Fairall, Pennie Hawkins, Bernice Ingram, Marion James, Mary Phillips, Linda Robertson, Lucy Trembath, Ann Wren and Ruth White. Thank you to Kate Buller of Rowan Yarns and Colinette Sainsbury of Colinette Yarns for letting me loose on their beautiful innovative fibers.

It has been a pleasure to collaborate with my friends Amy Carroll and Denise Brown. Thanks also to Emily Cook and Louise Dixon of Carroll and Brown for orchestrating the production.

Carroll and Brown Publishers would like to thank:
The Mayhew Animal Home (www.mayhewanimalhome.org) for their assistance with this project.
Production Karol Davies
IT Paul Stradling
Photographic Assistant David Yems

SUPPLIERS

Rowan/Jaeger (USA)
4 Townsend West, Suite 8,
Nashua, New Hampshire
03064 USA
Tel (603) 886 5041/5043
wfibers@aol.com

Colinette Yarns (USA)
Unique Kolours
Tel (800) 25-2DYE 4
www.uniquekolours.com
uniquekolo@aol.com

Sasha Kagan
www.sashakagan.com
sasha@sashakagan.com